Land Your Dream Career in College

Land Your Dream Career in College

The Complete Guide to Success

Tori Randolph Terhune and Betsy A. Hays

ROWMAN & LITTLEFIELD
Lanham • Boulder • New York • London

Published by Rowman & Littlefield
A wholly owned subsidiary of The Rowman & Littlefield Publishing Group, Inc.
4501 Forbes Boulevard, Suite 200, Lanham, Maryland 20706
www.rowman.com

Unit A, Whitacre Mews, 26-34 Stannary Street, London SE11 4AB, United Kingdom

Distributed by NATIONAL BOOK NETWORK

British Library Cataloguing in Publication Information Available

The hardback edition of this book was previously cataloged by the Library of Congress as follows:

Terhune, Tori Randolph.
  Land your dream career : eleven steps to take in college / Tori Randolph Terhune and Betsy A. Hays.
    p. cm.
  Includes index.
  1. College graduates—Employment. I. Hays, Betsy A. II. Title.
  HD6277.T46 2013
  650.14—dc23   2012045227

ISBN 978-1-4422-1947-2 (pbk. : alk. paper) — ISBN 978-1-4422-4663-8 (electronic)

♾™ The paper used in this publication meets the minimum requirements of American National Standard for Information Sciences—Permanence of Paper for Printed Library Materials, ANSI/NISO Z39.48-1992.

Printed in the United States of America

CONTENTS

PREFACE TO THE PAPERBACK EDITION

Congratulations!

You are someone who is poised to have a fabulous career. How do we know? You are reading this book. People who read things to better themselves tend to be the folks who are open to implementing good advice, which puts them ahead of the pack. And luckily, our readers have validated this idea with their terrific feedback about this book.

Whether you bought this book yourself, were given it as a gift, or checked it out from the library—it doesn't matter. What matters is that you have chosen to invest in *you*, and you have chosen to be even more fabulous than you are right this minute. Kudos!

In the time since we wrote this book, a few things have changed in the job search landscape. The economy is improving, making your opportunity outlook a little sunnier than those who were in your shoes just a few short years ago. Also, online personal brands have become an even bigger player in the job search areas of recruiting, hiring, and promotions.

These changes mean that the content of this book is even more relevant and necessary now. As you go through its pages, here are some things to keep in mind to help you make the right choices to get the most out of the current environment.

1. Your brand is your golden ticket.

Whether you interpret this as a Willy Wonka or American Idol metaphor, the meaning is the same. Without a solid, positive personal brand (your "golden ticket"), you can't get to your goal location. Pay close attention to our brand assessment in chapter 2 and note that everything you do affects the brand that you work to design, build, and protect. Take the time to do your own assessment and use your brand words (as you'll learn in chapter 2) as your guide as you complete the book. Also, make sure you offer the world a clear brand. As you may know from your own experience, people either ignore or become confused by things that are unclear.

2. Practice now to achieve perfection (or close to it!).

As you go through this book, embrace the sections that make you a better networker and practice them as you go along. For example, conduct an informational interview right after your read about it and the instructions are still fresh in your brain. Doing so will be helpful practice and make it easier to implement. After the first interview, schedule another one. Hint: Continue to practice and you'll see that the best way to build your network is slowly and gradually. Step by step. It's a marathon, not a sprint.

Another example is to develop your elevator pitch(es) as soon as you read about them, and then refine them as you read on and find tips that may help improve them. You can also set up (or complete and optimize) your LinkedIn profile as you read through chapter 9 (about new media and online tools). Practicing the tactics we offer in each chapter while still reading the content will not only help you get started on your career path as soon as possible but also confirm that you are able to adequately digest every piece of advice.

3. Social media can help you.

You'll read about social media in detail in chapter 9, so make sure you become active on at least one social network to build your personal brand and establish yourself in your industry. You can grow your network quickly via social media, and you can impress people quickly as well. We now recommend actively managing two or three networks where potential employers can find you—the good stuff about you, that is! Even if you are not into social media or don't see how to use it for your career launch, pay close attention to chapters 9 and 10. And please don't skip these sections if you think you are a digital expert. We promise that there is always something new to learn, especially when it comes to reframing how you use these tools to help you land your dream career.

4. Social media can harm you.

We hope this isn't news to you, but even if you've heard it before, please don't ignore this truth. Professionals around the world have lost their jobs or potential opportunities due to online faux pas. Audit your past posts and ask yourself, *would I want a potential boss or recruiter to read this post?* If not, rewrite (edit) or delete it. Overall, it is time to reform your outlook on the purpose of social media—even at this early stage of your career. The more you think of social networking as solely a brand-building opportunity, the faster you will advance and thrive professionally. It is not just your friends who read your posts and see your pictures—even if you have strict privacy settings and only close friends. Recruiters are smart and resourceful when it comes to social media, and they often find what you don't want them to find. So post carefully and strategically. Go on the offensive and only post content that will make people want to hire you. Now, you may think that we have just "sucked all the fun out of social media" (which we have been accused of), but we haven't. Take the opportunity to use your social media responsibly, and then use the texting photo option on your phone more frequently, as some things are better for sharing than posting. There is a difference! By the time you're done with this book, you'll really be a pro at this.

5. Standing out is the key to getting in.

Your competition is global and fierce. Choose to be empowered by this fact, not afraid. Let the competition fuel you and inspire you to be an even better version of yourself. Carefully weigh all of the ideas we present and select the ones that make the most sense for *you*. Finding the few areas where you can excel and contribute (rather than trying to be good at everything) is key to charting the course to your dream career. We talk more about this fact in chapter 10, but it applies throughout the entire book (especially when we talk about your personal brand builders and killers). We can't emphasize enough that if you apply all of our brand-building suggestions, you *will* stand out in the best possible way. We promise.

Please remember that your time in college is all about maximizing your time as a student and making the most of the opportunities that you *only* have while in college. However, these are also important years in your life that you only get to live once. We've included sections on creating wiggle room and taking time for celebration on purpose, as your college career should also be filled with fun and adventure—which you won't have time for unless you choose to create time for it.

We wish you nothing but the very best as you land your dream career!
Tori and Betsy

ACKNOWLEDGMENTS

W e have so many thanks to give! Huge, heartfelt thank yous to our wonderful agent, Anne Develin, and our publisher, Rowman & Littlefield Publishers, Inc., and all of our great editors, idea-bouncer-offers, and supporters, including Tori's parents, John and Melanie, and Betsy's mom, Nancy, as well as Angie Tarr, Jan Edwards, Kim Mooney, Merrilee Montgomery, Dr. Roberta Asahina, Dr. Susan Sivek, C. J. Randolph, Joe Prior, Mari and Dave Terhune, Anne McClintic, Kimberlee Peyret, Reganie Smith-Love, Megan Lerma, the students in the Fall 2011 "PR Writing" class at Fresno State, and the many students who lent their personal stories to our book. And, of course, our fantastic families—Tori's husband, David, and Betsy's husband, Brad, and her daughters, Sam and Jackie.

Thank you all from the bottom of our hearts!
—*Tori and Betsy*

INTRODUCTION

Tori Randolph Terhune and Betsy A. Hays

Many college students walk across the stage at graduation expecting to be hired shortly thereafter, because growing up they were promised that if they got a degree, they would get a great job. Unfortunately, for many college graduates, this is not the case. Getting a job after college does not depend solely on the grades you receive or the fact that you have a degree. The professional landscape has changed, and companies want proven, experienced employees in their workforce. This book will help you utilize available tools and strategies to take full advantage of opportunities that are only presented to students.

Land Your Dream Career in College: The Complete Guide to Success will demonstrate how you can efficiently use your time on campus to start building a successful career as early as your freshman year. We will lead you carefully and strategically through eleven steps designed to help you set yourself up for success, without focusing on grades or papers. To provide you with the full advantage of reading a book written by *both* a recent college graduate and a college professor, we provide distinct authorship of the chapters (i.e., chapter 1 is written by Tori, chapter 2 by Professor Hays, etc.). We coauthor two chapters as well, providing you with our joint perspectives in the areas of new and social media and in utilizing all of the book's tools to the best of your ability.

The steps—presented in a concise, easy-to-digest way—include tips on becoming an expert in your field, building your brand, getting involved in and outside the classroom, allowing for wiggle room, networking, following the 75/25 rule (75 percent thinking, 25 percent doing), and using new media (including social networking and blogging) to launch your career. Chapters include tips, notes, stories, and mini case-study examples of the steps being used successfully.

At the end of each chapter you will find a cheat sheet summary of the chapter. You can use these cheat sheets to refresh your memory and see if there are certain points you want to go back and delve into again.

Before we begin, we'd like to share with you why we wrote this book.

Tori

As a recent college graduate (California State University, Fresno, May 2009), I witnessed most of my peers entering the "real world" with little to no experience, poorly filled résumés, and no job prospects. By the time I graduated, I had three years of relevant work experience, five completed internships, two start-up businesses, more than twenty articles published in newspapers and magazines, the Central California Rookie of the Year title from the Central California Chapter of the Public Relations Society of America, and a full-time job waiting for me. While still a student, I guest lectured several times for classes in my department and was honored at graduation as the Outstanding Public Relations Student. My peers asked me for letters of recommendation for their interviews, and I helped many students launch their job searches. None of this was by accident. I had a strategy from day one and set my priorities accordingly. I worked diligently in my classes and achieved good grades, but my focus was getting my career started early (i.e., while I was still in school). My plan worked so well that I wanted to share this knowledge with you.

Professor Hays

For the last fourteen years I have taught in the mass communication and journalism department at California State University, Fresno. In addition to coordinating our department-wide internship program, I also teach the public relations and media ethics courses. As a college professor and a self-proclaimed "success junkie," I have always focused on helping my students succeed. Over the years, through my own experiences and through those of my students, clients, and colleagues, I have collected a set of practices and behaviors that enable people to set themselves up for success. This book is the collaboration of tried and true practices that Tori and I both use to thrive. And they have helped others thrive as well—especially college students like you.

Now let's get started . . .

CHAPTER ONE
START NOW
Tori

A Story

Christy came to campus as a college freshman already feeling behind the curve. She grew up in a small, rural farm-working community that lacked many basic resources, and she felt that high school hadn't adequately prepared her for her future. However, because she was a go-getter, Christy decided to get ahead of the game and get involved as much as she could, soaking up every last bit of knowledge available to her in college. Her freshman year she took a few introductory classes that were related to her interests, and she immediately fell in love with her major, public relations.

When Christy reviewed the catalog requirements for her major, she noticed that she would need to complete an internship. She spoke with an advisor who asked her to take a few more classes before trying to get out in the community, but that didn't stop Christy. She marched over to a community center in a neighboring town and offered to volunteer as an intern to get experience. By the beginning of her sophomore year she had her first "real" internship and took every class as early as she could.

"In my sophomore year I joined our university's student-professional organization, the Public Relations Student Society of America, and the on-campus student-operated PR firm," says Christy. "I was the youngest in the firm and felt like I needed to work twice as hard to keep up. Taking classes early and being surrounded by upperclassmen was really a motivator for me. I just felt

4

the need to get involved in anything I could. I knew that everything I'd need wouldn't be in a textbook. It just doesn't work that way."

Christy believed that a mix of her classes, internships, and hands-on, real-world experience would be the way to be successful. Completely focused on what she needed to get done, it wasn't until junior year that Christy looked up and realized she was well ahead of her classmates. She went on to land a job in public health as a regional media and communications coordinator—just in time for graduation!

Christy isn't the only one with a story like this. When I talk to students who are set on their career paths before graduation, the common factors are that they started building their knowledge base and getting experience as early as possible. Throughout this book there will be many stories like hers from other students, myself, and Professor Hays to help show you how to apply the theories and steps in this book. Below are the first few tips to help you get on your way.

Decide What You Want to Do

(If you've already decided on a major and started your career path, you may skip to the next section.)

It doesn't matter if you are a senior in college or a senior in high school: It's never too early to start figuring out what you want to do with your life. You can do this via high school electives or by researching different colleges and what they offer. In fact, basing your college decision on which universities have the majors you are interested in (or have stellar departments for your interests) is one of the best decisions you can make. That means that when you are still in high school or at a community college you should tour campuses that have the program(s) you are interested in and speak with members of the department and, if possible, a few of the students. Find out what you like and don't like about several different schools, and weigh the pros and cons of each. Picking your college is a major life decision. I can't stress how important it is not to follow all of your friends. I promise you will make new friends, so please pick your school based on studies.

5

But don't fret if you are already in college and didn't pick your university based on your interests or if you're unsure what you want to study. Just start now and decide what you want to do.

Read the Class Schedule or General Catalog

Go online or go to the bookstore and familiarize yourself with the classes you will need to take, and make sure they sound interesting to you. For example, if you want to go into hospitality, many universities will have you take wine and beer classes (which sounds like a blast!), but you'll also have to take restaurant safety courses with a lot of testing. The bottom line? Don't pick a major based solely on one class you think would be fun. You can always take that class as an elective, along with your required major coursework.

While looking at the different classes you might take, consider where your talents lie. Ask trusted family members and friends what they think you're good at, and try a few of those options out. For example, when I started college my dad thought I would make a great engineer because I did well in math classes, but my mom said I should write. And in the end I decided I prefer words over math.

Realize that when you make the decision to pursue a major you're in it for the long haul. You'll want to enjoy the classes you're studying for all day and night. See if there are any tests or special requirements that need to be taken care of in order to fulfill the major, and note when they need to be handled.

Take a Few Introductory Classes

Once you've found a course of study that you think you can stick with and be passionate about, take an introductory class. Make sure you like the instructor, the way the class flows, and the amount of work asked of you. It's also important to make sure you agree with the ideologies discussed and that you enjoy the way the material is presented (i.e., you aren't falling asleep). Realize that many departments only have a few instructors, so you may be stuck with the same professor in several classes.

TIP: Sites like RateMyProfessors.com are a great resource to finding out which instructors you should take when signing up for classes. You can search by college, department, and name of professor to find ratings and comments made by other students. Most students leave very specific tips, including how many papers and tests you have to take in each class, how to study for them, and the amount of homework you should expect.

What should you do if you really love a certain major but can't stand the department or professors at your university? Consider switching departments to do something similar (i.e., journalism instead of English, or physics instead of mechanical engineering—oddly enough, the applications of these are very similar and can lead to very similar jobs). If you're stuck or just completely sold on your major, consider transferring to a different university. It may sound a tad dramatic, but I really want to stress the importance of enjoying your major and department. It will be very difficult to apply many of the theories in this book if you can't stand your professors or don't enjoy the material in your courses.

Can't decide between a few different majors? Take the introductory course in several different areas to get a feel for what you'd like best.

A Story

I started college as a communication major. Many of the communication courses were general education requirements, so I happened to take a few in my first two semesters in school. The classes were okay, but I didn't feel extremely passionate about anything in them, and the peers I took the courses with seemed uninterested and bored. My second semester I also took a beginning course in mass communication and journalism, which I realized was very interesting to me, and I loved the professor. The overarching department was very large, so I still needed to make a decision between what interested me: advertising, public relations, or journalism. I took courses in each (making my advertising course count toward the general electives I needed and the journalism course count toward a class I would need for the major). I fell in love with the public relations courses (and met my fabulous coauthor, Professor Hays). I was sold. I continued to work on my journalism skills to help my overall writing but did so outside of class as a freelancer to keep from putting too much on my academic plate (and also get paid). After experimenting in all the areas, I knew that I had picked the right major for me, and I've never looked back.

Just like I did, it's okay to try out a few different major options in the beginning, but keep it to three or four different departments, if possible. And then try to make the introductory classes count for general education or elective credits as well. That way you can both eliminate some options and get the credits you need to graduate on time. Remember, you want to stay on track to graduate as soon as possible so you can start that career.

Tip: Another great way to decide between career choices is to check starting salary ranges in different areas for the careers you're interested in. Sites like Monster.com are great for this purpose. Look up a few of your possible career paths, and then decide if you love something that will also pay you well.

Develop a Plan of Attack

Once you've taken a few introductory classes and have an idea of what you want to do in your career, start taking advantage of class-planning options at your university.

Be Strategic

When you've decided on your major, make an appointment with your assigned advisor as soon as possible. Get to know him or her, and make sure he or she knows who you are. If you don't think your advisor can really help you, if he or she seems to not be knowledgeable about your major requirements or seems to not care about whether or not you graduate on time, it might be worth it to consider switching advisors. Check your department's policy and, if possible, speak to another advisor, asking if they would direct you to a strategic four-year plan to graduate.

Work with your advisor to plan which classes you need to take and when, because some classes have prerequisites and some are only offered during certain quarters and semesters. For example, my major had three core classes you had to take, but Class 1 had to be completed the semester before Class 2, and Class 2 before Class 3; you couldn't take them concurrently. Some students realized they had all three classes left in their senior year and had to stay an extra semester to finish their requirements to graduate. Too many students stay in school longer than they need to because they don't check prerequisites and plan their schedules accordingly.

TIP: If you meet with your advisor and let them know how excited you are to get your classes going and get started working in the real world, they just might allow you to take classes early.

While developing your coursework plan, you'll probably notice that it's best to start taking basic major-required classes early, mixed with your general electives. No matter what your university says, it's not smart to take only general education courses first. You'll thank yourself for this later when you can mix your tougher major classes with easier, less intensive general education classes. Balance is the key to not overwhelming yourself. Also, the earlier you learn the basics of your major, earn the credits, and get the practice, the earlier you can start volunteering, interning, and working in your field of choice.

You'll also want to plan ahead to graduate with a few extra units. *Never* try to graduate with the exact amount of credits needed to walk across the stage. If, for whatever reason, something happens in one of your senior courses and you don't pass, it's an extra semester for you in school.

Be Proactive

Be proactive with your advisor and peers. Make yourself known to them and everyone else in the department. You never know who can help you or serve as a reference, and the more people you have on your side, the better. Plus advisors and professors have the insider information and can caution you if there are any changes in the department that might keep you from completing your classes as planned. If you're on their mind, they'll be sure to remember to let you know when these situations arise.

Another way you can get involved with advisors or professors is to offer to do an independent study with them. This can be anything to help that professor and get a little bit of credit, increase your network, and build your reputation in your department, as well as expand your breadth of work. For example, I wrote articles for local newspapers and magazines and earned class credit but never had to attend an actual class. A fellow student helped an art teacher with art projects outside of class and received credit as well. Independent study can be very beneficial if you have a busy schedule and need flexibility earning credits. Generally these independent studies can be on your own time and sometimes even from your dorm room or apartment. Plus, when you need a letter of recommendation, you'll have a glowing one from the advisor or professor you assisted.

And don't forget your peers. They will be wonderful resources and partners for you as you work through your major coursework. Some people like study buddies, and some don't, but having people to call for clarification or collaboration is always a good idea. Be proactive and get to know them as soon you can in entry-level classes. Remember that you'll be in classes together for a few years. If they've taken other classes before you, they can give you some much-needed knowledge and advice (i.e., the professor pulls exam questions straight from the book or only from the lecture).

Be Diligent

As mentioned earlier, the worst thing that can happen when you think you're two semesters from graduating is finding out that one little prerequisite or overlooked class puts you back another semester. I've seen this happen countless times, and not only is it disappointing, but it also wastes a lot of time and money—and puts your big-time career on hold for another few months. Don't let the small stuff set you back. Take control of your schedule and requirements, and track everything you're taking against the general catalog requirements and with your advisor.

This doesn't mean walking into the advisor's office one time to set up your plan and then assuming you're good to go for all four years: Departments are constantly changing the quarters or semesters in which classes are offered, prerequisites, or when you need to take a class, among countless other things.

TIP: Some classes and majors even have writing or math test requirements that you may not know about until you try to register for the course. Be clear with your advisor that there can be no roadblocks to you taking your classes, and set up when you should take each of these tests as soon as possible.

How do you stay in the know? Meet with your advisor once per quarter or semester to stay on track. Walk in with your proposed schedule for the next few quarters or semesters, and ask for his/her opinion. Always speak to your advisor before you register for your next classes to make sure you catch any issues before you've set your schedule.

Don't trust others when it comes to your degree. While your advisor is a fantastic resource for you as you learn how to schedule courses and what your requirements are, he/she is not the final say when it comes to whether you get your degree. Be sure to take the advice in stride, but always triple-check your requirements yourself. If your advisor makes a mistake, he/she isn't the one harmed—you are. So take responsibility for your own degree, and make sure you understand how everything works so you can be sure to graduate on your time line.

A Story

Taylor was on track to graduate, had met with her advisor her senior year, and was ready to go to graduate school to earn her teaching credential. After she was accepted into graduate school and had walked across the stage at graduation, she learned from her department that she hadn't actually graduated—she was short one credit. Not only was this annoying, because it meant she would have to go back in the fall to spend quite a bit more money to take one unit, but her graduate school also threatened to throw her out before she even started because people on the wait-list had met all of their graduation requirements. Keep in mind that she followed all the rules, her advisor had told her she was ready to graduate, and her school didn't even catch the error until they were about to send her a diploma. Luckily, she was able to work out a solution with her advisor by counting an internship as credit, but it was a huge scare and a lot of extra work she didn't need to go through post–graduation party. Don't let this happen to you; be diligent and take responsibility for your own fate.

Always Think about How Your Actions Now Impact Your Future Career

For each of the above steps, and in every class you take, always think about how your actions might impact your future. Getting your major classes done early leads to more chances to work in the real world. And working closely with your professors or advisor leads to stellar letters of recommendation and possibly a lifelong mentor (or even a coauthor for a future book).

Part of successfully launching your career is getting started as soon as possible. Set your strategic plan, proactively check for holes in your plan, and diligently track your requirements to stay on course and get that dream career!

Cheat Sheet

- Decide what you want to do.
  - Read the semester's class schedule or general catalog.
  - Take a few introductory classes.

- Develop a plan of attack.
  - Be strategic.
  - Be proactive.
  - Be diligent.

- Always think about how your actions now impact your future career.

CHAPTER TWO

DESIGN, BUILD, AND PROTECT YOUR BRAND

Professor Hays

Right now is the perfect time for you to create your professional brand. The world hasn't seen that much of you yet (unless you were a famous child actor), and college is the place where people expect you to "find yourself."

Where to Begin

Start by writing down as many adjectives as you can that either (1) describe the best of you now or (2) describe the best of how you want to be. Make this list as long as possible. Take several days to complete it. Work on it. Take a break. Then work on it again. Then look at the list, and group ideas together. Eliminate words that mean the same thing to you, leaving the strongest word. Then narrow the list down to three or four words total. This might be hard, as you'll want to keep *all* your beautiful words. But you can't. You are choosing the core of your professional brand, and the core can't be made up of everything. Four is the *maximum*, and three is the *minimum* for this exercise. You'll probably end up with a combination of both words that describe what you are most proud of and words that represent who you are on your way to becoming.

For example, right now I have four words that define my brand. I say "right now" because, like me, your words will evolve as your brand and career do. Things that are important now might not be later, and vice versa. While your core brand will probably remain the same, it will fine-tune itself over time. Here are my words:

1. *Polished.* To me, being polished encompasses many things: looking professional, being calm and assertive, and sharing that you can handle the things that life throws your way.

2. *Positive.* I believe wholeheartedly that attitude *is* everything, and being positive has done wonderful things for my career and my life.

3. *Professional.* Because I am a professor, I am a role model. I can never forget that. Also, the idea of being a professional encompasses a lot of things I value deeply—solid ethics, extreme competence, flawless dependability, and so forth.

4. *Fun.* This one is simple—and important, due to my desire for balance, as I believe it is important to be fun.

And, because I know you are curious, Tori's words are as follows:

1. *Motivated.* She is a self-starter with ambition. She's goal-oriented and focused on moving toward accomplishment, whatever that entails.

2. *Compassionate.* This is one of her core values as both a person and professional. Tori believes that you never know where the other person is coming from, or what kind of day they had, so your first response should be compassionate listening, not knee-jerk reactions and anger.

3. *Quick study.* She picks up things faster than most and completes work quickly and efficiently. (In fact, this was the topic of one of our first professional conversations, as she was struggling with charging a client by the hour, because she felt that her ability to work quickly would harm her ability to be paid a fair price for the project. She decided to charge a fair project fee instead, and both she and the client ended up satisfied with the price.)

4. *Proactive.* She has great initiative, with the ability to always see what needs to be done and then make it happen. This is another key to her career success and also a way that *you* can set yourself apart from others. Being proactive is discussed in detail in chapter 4's section on being a problem solver, not a problem identifier. Stay tuned.

What to Do Next

Once you have your brand words, the words that describe the core of your professional brand, you need to start building that brand by showing the world that you *are* those words. Ultimately, you want people to repeatedly use those words to describe you; these are the things you want people to say when they are talking about you when you're not in the room! That is when you know you have succeeded in building your brand.

For starters, ask yourself if others would use those words to describe you right now. If not, please don't panic. Just know those are the things you will have to work hardest on. If the answer is a resounding yes, or if you can answer yes to some of them, then these are the things you will just need to maintain.

NOTE: Just because the idea of maintenance sounds easy, please don't take this for granted. Maintenance, while clearly not as difficult as building from scratch, is just as important, if not more so. For example, your hair probably doesn't cause you too much trouble unless you skip a scheduled haircut or two. Your teeth are probably similar. Keeping your regular haircut and dentist appointments is not hard, but if you skip them, all kinds of trouble follows. If you work hard to either get in good physical shape or lose some weight, you can't just stop all effort and call it done. You must keep exercising to maintain your fitness level, and you must keep eating healthily if you want to keep your weight where you'd like it to be. Just so, time spent on maintenance saves the much harder work of starting from scratch later.

Build Your Brand Every Day

Now that you have an idea of what your brand is, you can start to build it.

Be Congruent

The best way to do so is to be congruent. I love this word—it's just about the only math concept that I have always kept with me. Its best definition comes from its relation to geometry, where it means *coinciding at all points when superimposed* (thank you, Dictionary.com!). In other words, everything has to match up. This means simply that 100 percent of the time, both personally and professionally, your actions *must* match your words. If they don't, people will stop believing you. You'll be the boy who cried wolf, and when you do actually mean what you say, no one will listen. Some call this "walking the talk."

The fastest way to lose your credibility is by being incongruent. And credibility, if we are all honest about it, is the only real currency we have for success in life. It is easy to lose and really difficult, if not impossible, to get back.

Just like your socks should match, so should the rest of you—meaning that who you are and what you say you're about should be apparent in the way you behave. Think about it: You probably know someone who always talks about how organized they are or how punctual they are, but when you look at their behavior, it doesn't match their "talk." So you "believe" their behavior, as you should, and don't think of them as either organized or punctual. That is how it works. Frankly, we should be grateful life works this way, because we don't have to go around telling people that our brand is "W, X, Y, and Z"—all we have to do is be W, X, Y, and Z, and it will become our brand.

You might even consider writing down your brand words and keeping them visible to you. This will encourage you to act these words and not just talk about them. If "strong writer" is part of your brand, be a strong writer. If "fashionable" is part of your brand, be fashionable. Don't talk about it—do it!

A Story

I was driving home from work one day, and I came up behind a car with rosary beads hanging from the rear-view mirror and one of those fish stickers that represents Christianity. I then saw another sticker, which made me chuckle. It said, "My kid can kick your honor student's ass." Funny? Perhaps. But it is also a wonderful example of incongruence.

People will believe our brand when our words and deeds match. It's as simple as that. But, as with all things of value and importance, this is much harder to implement in practice. However, I know you are committed to building a strong brand, and I am sure that you want to be successful, so I know you'll try harder than the person who was driving that car.

Some of you deep-thinking types might dismiss the story above, insisting that it is more of an example of how complex our personalities are in reality. Point taken, but we are talking about building your brand, and the world doesn't have time to learn about all of your complexities. It needs to absorb the most prominent things about you, decide whether or not to engage with you, and move on. Your complexities need to be saved for those you are closest to.

A Sigh of Relief

Now I'm going to share something with you that will probably bring a sigh of relief. Perhaps the thought of consistently building your brand every day by *being* your brand every day is a little overwhelming and potentially exhausting. If it's *really* overwhelming, you might need to choose a brand that is more authentic to who you actually are. It shouldn't be that hard, but feeling a little overwhelmed is normal at this point. So, you'll be happy to know that *consistency is more important than perfection.*

That's right. You don't have to be perfect.

Relieved? I thought so! (And, frankly, so are we.)

You do have to be as consistent as you possibly can, every day. But you don't have to be perfect. Some days you are going to be a little off, and you won't be your entire brand. And some days you might not be any of your brand. But most days, you need to be most of it, and on even more days you need to be all of it. This is how you succeed in this venture.

The key message here is to not beat yourself up if you aren't a perfect brand builder every day. We are only human, after all.

The Basics for Any Good Brand

Regardless of what your brand words are, the following are some tips that I have found help anyone have a strong brand. I get asked to give presentations and workshops on this content all the time on campus, as it really resonates with people like you, the college student.

Dress How You Want to Be Treated—Like a Professional

Always dress in a way that builds your brand. Be modest, clean, and put-together.

Okay, you might be thinking that I'm just bringing this up because I'm not twenty years old and am a mother of two daughters. While all of that is true, it's not why this rule is included. It's included because at least once a month, and sometimes more often, an internship supervisor or business leader or someone I meet while out in the community complains to me about two things regarding college students.

This is the first one. (The second one is the next part of this section.) These people pull me aside at functions and say to me, "Betsy, you've got to talk to them about how to dress. What are these girls thinking when they come to an interview with cleavage showing and super-tight clothing and extremely short skirts?"

So this is me talking to you, ladies, about how to dress. Here is the bottom line: Regardless of how darling you think you are, and regardless of the way people dress on TV, in the actual real world you live and want to work in, it is not professional or a good idea to show your cleavage or your muffin top or any part of your thong.

Guys, you're not exempt from this, either, though the ladies tend to get more of the heat, rightly or wrongly. Be sure you look clean, pressed, and presentable (and pull up your pants).

Fair or not, in the professional world your grooming matters.

Become a Solid Writer

This is the other complaint that many people have about college students and young professionals. Therefore, I encourage you to do whatever it takes to make yourself a solid writer. Frankly, it doesn't matter what profession you are in. Good writers get better jobs, get promoted faster, and make more money. In fact, I talked to a professional colleague while writing this chapter who agreed that if a new graduate is a great writer, even in this tough economy, that student will always be employable.

Whenever you can (fairly easily) obtain a skill that not many others have, you make yourself more marketable and a more attractive hire. So do it. Take lots of writing classes from the business and journalism departments. This is where you'll learn the kind of concise and to-the-point writing that you need to succeed in any field. (Obviously, if you want to be a creative writer, there are different classes you need to take as well.)

In fact, everyone should write for their college newspaper or website. The option is usually open to all majors, and this is a built-in writing clinic at your fingertips. They will guide you, edit your work, and help you become a better writer. In fact, they have to—otherwise the paper will be terrible, and no one wants that.

Be Articulate with a Good Vocabulary

Being a good verbal communicator is also a skill that can set you apart, make you more marketable, and get you promoted faster. Having the ability to be articulate is a lovely thing to be born with, and some people are, but it's also a skill you can learn. And you learn it through practice.

Put yourself in positions where you have to speak, explain, or persuade. This will make you a better communicator. Be an officer in a club. Volunteer to be a team leader in class. Join some committees.

Just as important as practice is observation and modeling. Watch people who are articulate. Listen to what they say and how they say it. Model this, and you will be articulate too.

A Story

During my first staff meeting at my first "big girl" job, I was terrible. I rambled, spoke too quickly, and pretty much was a disaster. Right afterward, my supervisor pulled me aside and said, "You need to watch [the big bosses] next time during the staff meeting. Be like them, and you'll go places." So I watched them. I learned to speak more slowly, use more eye contact and hand gestures, and increase the words in my vocabulary. I haven't been embarrassed at a staff meeting since. (Oh, unless you count the time that I spilled an entire glass of ice water on my new department chair's carpet the first day I met her. True story. See? Nobody's perfect!)

Vocabulary is important. We all should use more of the English language than we do. For one thing, doing so makes people think we are smarter (bonus!). For another, we have more ways to communicate effectively when we have more word choices. I'm not talking about using a fourteen-syllable words that no one understands. People who use those types of words all the time are annoying and are rarely good communicators. But expanding your vocabulary and tossing out an occasional word that is not used very often is a certain brand builder. Here's a trick that might help you feel more comfortable with this idea. When you use what my mom always calls a "fifty-cent word," call attention to it. "Hey, I love that word, don't you? It means [definition]. I just learned it yesterday."

While we're on the subject of vocabulary, I need to tell you (although you probably already know) that if you have a "like" or "I'm all" or "you know" issue with your speech, now is the time to fix it. I have students with this issue, and in one conversation I had while writing this chapter, a student used "like" in *every* sentence. It was very distracting. And, just as having a good vocabulary makes people think you are smarter, using "like" and "I'm all, he's all, she's all" frequently makes people think you are dumb. (I know this is harsh, but it is also true.) Start fixing it, now, and increase the value of your brand.

Be Four Minutes Early to Everything

Punctuality is something else that you can do to set yourself apart from most other people on the planet, particularly among people your age.

In order to really "get" why this is a big deal, I want you to think about all of the messages that you send people when you are late to an appointment, interview, or meeting. Write down five adjectives that describe what people think about folks who are late. Be brutal, because that's the reality. Now look at that list. Would you like to include any of those words at the top of your résumé? I'm assuming not. However, when you are late, this is exactly what you are doing. Think about it.

So, my advice is for you to be four minutes early for everything. More than that could actually be annoying—both to you and to the person you are meeting. Four minutes gives you a tiny cushion if you need it, and if this is your habit, you will be perceived as more dependable, organized, brilliant, reliable, focused, and committed than anyone else. Become a model of punctuality. Be the person that makes other people be on time because they *know* that you will be there on time and they don't want to inconvenience you.

Be Ridiculous about Gratitude and Circling Back

I chose the word *ridiculous* carefully, because it describes exactly the point I want to convey. I really do encourage you to be *ridiculous* about gratitude. Become the "thank you" king or queen. Everyone likes to be thanked. Being appreciated is one of life's most satisfying elements. And when we are thanked when we aren't expecting it, it's even more special.

Sending a thank you note also gives you a chance to circle back. This keeps everyone on task, as your circle-backs should include what any next steps are for everyone involved. This holds everyone (including you) accountable and clears up any misconceptions or fuzziness. You should thank and circle back with

- People you meet who can build your network. "So enjoyed meeting you. Thank you for your time and for telling me about . . . When you get a chance, please send me that . . . we discussed."

- People that you meet with. "Thank you for taking the time to meet with me. I think we made a lot of progress today. See you on [date]. Per our discussion, at that time you will . . . and I will . . . Thank you."

- Anyone who does something nice for you. "Thank you for . . . That was so kind [thoughtful, unexpected—whatever is appropriate . . .]."

How you thank people is up to you. I prefer e-mail, perhaps because it's the most efficient. Traditional mail is fine for big things (job or internship interviews, etc.), but for most occasions e-mail is fine. (In fact, because life moves so quickly these days, after an interview send both an e-mail and a note via regular mail to make sure your thanks arrive in time.) Sometimes, depending on your relationship with the person, a text or Tweet or Facebook message is a good way to go.

On my daily to-do list I have a line item that reads "Thank yous." Really, I do. Every afternoon (or almost every afternoon) I reflect on my day and send out a quick thank you e-mail to those I need to thank. Sometimes it's people I have met with. Sometimes it's someone who gave me some useful information or a lead. And, of course, if someone bought me coffee or lunch or did something kind, they get an e-mail as well. Some days it's just one e-mail. Some days it's ten. It takes just a few minutes, and it's 100 percent worth it.

Close Communication Loops

Another amazing way you can build your brand in a positive way is to close your communication loops. This is something else that will differentiate you from most people, especially people your age. When someone texts you, text them back. When someone calls you, call them back. When someone e-mails you, e-mail them back. Let people know their message was received. If you call or text or e-mail someone and ask them to do something and they do it, respond with "Thank you." If you are really happy about it, respond with "Thank you!"

If someone thanks you, however, you don't always have to say "You're welcome." Unless the communication loop starts with "Thank you," this phrase can be the end of the loop. *Not* closing communication loops causes problems and stress for those trying to communicate with you. They will wonder if you got the message. They will wonder if you are working on the task. Don't make people wonder. Close the loop—and you can even close it quickly with only one or two words. Here are some ideas:

- Sounds good.

- See you then.

- On it.

- Done.

- Will do.

Ideally, you want to close all communication loops in the same day, but within twenty-four hours is usually fine, and obviously if the communication is sent on a Friday, getting back to people on Monday is usually acceptable.

People who are responsive and courteous and thoughtful (which this strategy represents) are top-of-mind for all kinds of wonderful opportunities.

Post Carefully and Strategically

In chapter 9 we will detail specifics regarding new media tools, but posting online and via social media needs to be mentioned here as well. At this point, I'm just going to give you one simple rule:

Before you post anything anywhere, ask yourself, "Does this post build my brand?"

If it doesn't, don't post it. What goes onto the Internet stays on there forever, and you want to make sure you protect your online reputation with everything you've got. If you have something to share that doesn't build your brand, pick up the phone and call someone or send them a text. It will be out of your brain but not out on the Web.

Strive for HIC—Honesty, Integrity, and Credibility

As mentioned above, your credibility is your currency. It's how you'll get what you want, regardless of what that is. So don't mess with your credibility or put it in harm's way. *Ever.* Once it's gone, usually you can't get it back. And even if you can, it takes a really, really, really long time to do so, and it will never be the same as it was before.

So strive for HIC—be honest, have integrity, and you'll always enjoy credibility.

Lying sometimes appears easy at first, but it never ends up that way. And, as history (as well as current events) has proved, people usually get into *way* more trouble for covering things up than for whatever they did in the first place that they were trying to cover up.

So tell the truth. Even if it hurts—and we all know that sometimes it does! A lot!

Tell the truth, and then fix things if you need to, but always be straight up with folks, and your integrity and credibility will never be called into question. You will always enjoy wonderful relationships and tons of personal and professional success.

This sounds simple, and it is in concept, but not in practice—or else everyone would do it, right?

So now is your chance to not be like everybody else, which I know is your goal, or you wouldn't be reading this book. Especially given the current tough economy, it is not the time to fade into the woodwork, or, as my husband says, it's not the time to be the weakest link.

So stand out by striving for HIC—honesty, integrity, and credibility.

Customize

Now that I've shared some brand-building essentials, think about your specific brand. What behaviors do you need to choose that will help you build *your* brand? How can you show people that you are who you want to be? Notice I used the word *show* because, as you are aware, talk is cheap, and not nearly as helpful in brand building as behavior.

For us to believe it, you have to *be* it.

The rest of this book will help you on your path. Have fun, and good luck!

Brand-Building Bonus Section: Powerful Presentation Skills

Solid public speaking is also a terrific brand builder, so I've decided to include a section with some basics that will help you improve if you are currently a good speaker and get on your way if this is an area you struggle with. This could certainly be a book on its own, but we wanted to make sure you had some solid ideas *now* to help you move forward in this critical area. These skills will help you in any situation where you need to speak in front of others—whether it's in a class or a club meeting or a talk to dozens or hundreds or thousands.

Right off the bat I'll let you in on the two secrets of success: research and preparation. These are two things that, frankly, can help you succeed in all areas of your life.

But what should you research, and how do you prepare?

First, right when you are asked to speak, you must get *all* of the information regarding your presentation, before you start doing anything regarding content.

Step 1: Who

Make sure you know the answers to the following questions:

- *Who* are you speaking to?

- What is their background?

- How much do they know about the topic?

- What are they expecting from you?

Then you can tailor your presentation to the audience. You want to deliver, so you need to know what they want. Whether your audience is your professor (as in a speech assignment), your fellow club officers, your friends, or your boss, you must get a handle on their expectations, or you will not be able to be successful. You also need to know a little about them, as well as their level of knowledge on the topic. Do your research, and then reap the benefits!

Step 2: What

More questions to answer:

- *What* are you speaking about?

- What is the main topic?

- From which angle should you approach the discussion?

- What are your key messages?

Knowing these things will help you craft your speech. But don't start writing yet! There is much more to research. Read on.

Step 3: Where

- *Where* are you speaking?

- What is the room size and set-up?

- What technology is available for you to use? Can you bring your own?

Room set-up is a big deal, and feel free to move things around in a room if it is not set up the way you like it. Most people have no problem with that, and usually when you start moving things people will stand up and start helping you.

Step 4: When

- *When* are you speaking?

- What is the time of day?

- How long will you be speaking?

All of this is important, particularly the length of time you'll be speaking, because preparing for a five-minute presentation is different from preparing for an hour-long talk (and is sometimes harder). Time of day is also worth considering, as people are usually able to pay attention better in the morning and are often looking for a little humor or entertainment in talks that happen in the evening. Good food for thought.

Step 5: Why

- *Why* are you speaking?

- Why did they choose you?

The more you know about the answers to this question, the more you'll know about what the expectations are for your talk. And this will normally boost your confidence as well, which is always good!

Step 6: How

- *How* are you speaking?

- Alone?

- With a team?

- With a partner?

- With a panel?

- At a podium?

- With a microphone? What kind?

Believe it or not, sometimes people don't ask these questions, and then when they arrive for their talk, they are surprised by something that throws them off their game. Don't let this happen to you.

Next Steps

Now that we have the scoop, you can start crafting your presentation. Again, you can use some or all of these tips regardless of your speaking opportunity, and regardless of your audience size.

Confirm What You Want to Accomplish

Say to yourself, "After the presentation, my audience will . . ." Figure out what you want them to do. Once you know this, you can craft a talk to get them to do just that.

Have a Simple Organization Scheme

Some ideas:

- Problem/solution: Explain the problem, and then share your solution.

- Chronology: Talk about things in the order in which they occurred.

- Numbers: Discuss the five (or whatever number) tips, thoughts, strategies, key points, reasons, ideas, and so forth.

Open Strong

Don't talk about what happened to you prior to the talk. Don't say anything negative or anything that will lessen the value of your presentation. It is surprising how people will kill their credibility by saying things like the following:

- "I'll be brief" or "I'll make this short"

- "I'll hurry"

- "I know we all want to get to lunch, but . . ."

- "This is hard to do in this short time frame . . ."

- "I'm so nervous"

Continue Strong

Here are a few tips to keep you going strong throughout your presentation:

- Stand up! (Unless it's awkward.) Standing increases the value of what you are saying.

- Show your passion. If you don't care, no one else will either.

- Talk to a few folks ahead of time. This way you have "friends" to look at for smiles and nods.

- Don't assume you know who the decision-maker is. Treat everyone in the room the same.

- Make eye contact. Or if you don't like eyes, look at people's noses. No one will know the difference, and noses are never scary.

- Move with purpose if you want to move around and use more of the room, but no pacing back and forth. This is very distracting. You want people to focus on your beautiful words!

- Engage the audience.
  - Ask easy questions that they can nod or raise their hand to answer.
  - Relate key points to them and their circumstances.

- Create congruence between verbal and nonverbal messages.
  - If you are talking about squashing the competition, make a squashing motion with your hand.
  - Try to use gestures to punctuate your words.

End Strong

You've done well so far, so you want to make sure you end strong. When you wrap up, make sure that you recap your central points and include your call-to-action. Be sure to ask for whatever it is you want the audience to do. If you want them to vote, ask for their vote. If you want them to attend, ask for them to attend. Be sure you always tell them *how* to do what you want them to do. This increases the likelihood that they'll actually do it.

Wrap Up Strong

Your talk isn't over when you give your conclusion. People may have questions, so you don't want to fizzle at the end. Some tips:

- Don't relax until you are alone, out of the room. Stay "on."

- Thank the audience for spending time with you.

- Don't ask for questions immediately.
  - Ask the first one yourself: "We've talked about X; how many of you think you can use this? How?"

- Then ask for any other questions.
  - If no one has a question, ask another one yourself: "If I were you, I might want to also know . . ."

What to Wear

- Look the part.
  - Are you a student? Look like a student.
  - Are you a potential business owner? Look like that.

- Dress according to the occasion.

- Wear what looks good on *you* (colors, types of clothing, etc.).

- Use the Goldilocks analogy:
  - Your clothes shouldn't be too tight.
  - They shouldn't be too loose.
  - They should fit "just right."

- Test your clothing in a full-length mirror.

- Bottom line regarding what to wear: Your outfit should not detract from your message; it should add to it.

Overcoming Nervousness

I always like to talk about overcoming nervousness when I talk about powerful-presentation skills, so here are some tips to help you be the confident, wonderful speaker I know you are going to become. I call them my Top-Seven Anxiety Busters!

1. Develop a ritual. Do the same thing prior to each talk. Like an athlete before a game, the warm-up is what gets you focused and ready for the upcoming task.

2. Use mantras. Remind yourself that you deserve to be there. They chose you because you were right for the presentation. This is your time to shine!

3. Practice. Practice equals confidence, which is essential to great public speaking.

4. Visualize success. Envision yourself being successful, and you increase the likelihood of being successful.

5. Breathe, hold it, and then let it out. If you are nervous, take a deep breath, hold it for as long as you can, and then let it out. You can do this in a room full of people and no one will know. It's a great trick.

6. Remember that they want you to succeed. Your audience is on your side, and don't ever forget it. They want you to be good,

because they are sharing part of their life with you, and all of us want as much of our life as possible to be amazing. So, therefore, they are probably pulling for you more than you are.

7. Be yourself. Authenticity is key. If you talk with your hands, talk with your hands. If you hate skirts, don't wear a skirt. Be true to yourself, and you'll eliminate distractions that can harm your focus.

PowerPoint Tips

- Use 28-point font, minimum. This provides you with less space for words (a plus!) and ensures your audience can read your slides.

- Edit heavily. Use as few words as possible. Your slides should augment your talk, not be comprised of all of your thoughts.

- Set up bullets to come up one at a time. This is the most important tip I can give. Figure out how to do this so you are feeding your audience your information one piece at a time, and not shoving it all in their face at once. This also gives your slides the opportunity to be your talk outline, eliminating the need for annoying and distracting note cards.

- Get a clicker. This way you can advance your slides while not having to touch your computer. You can walk around the room (slowly) and use more nonverbal communication. And you aren't hunched over your keyboard, which is usually unattractive.

Cheat Sheet

- Begin with your brand words (three to four maximum).
  - Be those words every day.

- Be congruent, but note that consistency is more important than perfection.

- Employ proven brand builders:
  - Dress like the professional that you are.
  - Become a solid writer.
  - Be articulate with a good vocabulary.
  - Be four minutes early to everything.
  - Close communication loops.
  - Be ridiculous about gratitude and circling back.
  - Post carefully and strategically.
  - Strive for HIC—honesty, integrity, and credibility.

- Customize.

- Bonus Section: Powerful Presentation Skills
  - Find out the who, what, where, when, why, and how of your talk.
  - Confirm what you want to accomplish.
  - Have a simple organization scheme.
  - Start strong.
    - Just start talking!
  - Continue strong.
    - Look at their noses, not their eyes.
  - End strong.
    - Include your call-to-action and the how.
  - Wrap up strong.
    - Manage the Q & A with your own questions.
  - Wear something that adds to your message and doesn't detract from it.
  - Use our tips for overcoming nervousness.
    - Have a pregame warm-up ritual.
    - Use a mantra.
    - Practice.
    - Visualize success.
    - Breathe.
    - Remember that your audience is your ally.
    - Be yourself.
  - Maximize your PowerPoint.
    - Use 28-point font (minimum).
    - Edit heavily.

IMMERSE YOURSELF—INSIDE AND OUTSIDE THE CLASSROOM
Tori

Going to all of your classes, doing your homework, and studying for tests are great ways to make sure you get that great GPA. However, I'm going to tell you something that goes against a lot of what you've learned so far in school: Your GPA is not a key point of your résumé, nor will it be a major factor in your life a year past graduation. In fact, most professors will tell you that unless your GPA is outstanding, it doesn't even belong on your résumé. Two questions that are rarely asked of college graduates in most fields: (1) What was your GPA? (2) How long did it take you to graduate? If you can do the job you are being hired to do, these things are ironically more than likely irrelevant.

> Tip: If you are planning to get a master's or other degree after your life as an undergraduate, then your grades are more important. Still, make sure you spend your undergraduate years focusing not only on your grades but also on getting the edge by putting in time outside of the classroom.

Employers will first look at the jobs and internships you've held, how long you've held them, and other relevant responsibilities. Now this is not to say that you shouldn't focus on your grades—it would be tough for you to prove to a potential employer that you are a smart cookie with a 2.0.

Also, keep in mind that you are developing your work ethic and that your professors won't recommend you if you make no effort in their classes. The point is that the grades in every class you take should not be your first priority. If you are a physics major, don't stress over a bad grade in your nutrition general education course; that most likely won't come back to bite you. (Unless, of course, you want to be a healthy eater!) The point is, a lot of students graduate with honors and a great report card. The ones that are successful go a few steps further.

Immerse Yourself Inside the Classroom and on Campus

We'll start on campus. Focusing yourself on campus means making an effort in class and taking advantage of opportunities you only get as a student. While you are a student, professionals and people in the outside world love you. You are cute and shiny and full of promise. Most will want to do anything to help you. Take advantage of it!

A Story

When my friend Stephanie was a student she wanted to start her own fashion business. She wasn't sure how to set up her pricing structure, so she called some designers and asked for help—as a student. Each designer was very forthcoming and shared tips and tricks to help her get started. Imagine if she had waited until she graduated to make those calls. Competitors never give that kind of information to each other. It was simply her student status that helped her land the information. She is now a successful entrepreneur living in New York City—with international customers!

So let's get started on immersing yourself in the classroom and on campus while you're still a student.

Know Your Professors

It's the start of the school year, and you have your class schedule in hand. All those professors' names (as we discussed in chapter 1) are extremely important. These professors are your new best friends. Introduce yourself (ahead of time, if possible), and let them know you are excited about the course, ask any questions you have about the class, and tell them what your plans are. Most professors will be interested; there are, of course, the marginal professors that don't want the one-on-one time, but it never hurts to be friendly.

Tip: Read through each syllabus, and study what each professor's likes or dislikes are. Some professors prefer projects to be turned in with a blue report cover, others like red folders with a label on the front, and still others hate all the fuss and just want you to staple it. Some love e-mailed assignments, and some hate them (like Professor Hays). Late papers are death in some courses and not such a big deal in others. Pay attention to these little details, and try to stay on top of your professors' partialities; it can only help you and is worth the couple extra dollars and time to run to the office supply store to purchase what they like. In the classroom, they are the bosses, so you should follow their rules.

Once the professor knows you, it is much easier to be successful in the course. If it's a difficult class, go to their office hours and ask for help. Let them know you sincerely want to learn what they are teaching and want to improve your skills and knowledge. This can turn a C paper into an A paper very easily. But the inverse is also true: If you never attend class, showing up only to turn in your homework, take the midterm, and take the final, your professors will notice.

A Story

A fellow student, Thomas, had a professor who collected homework on Friday and handed it back on Monday. More than half of the class would only show up on Friday to drop off the homework and then leave right after, not even staying for that day's lecture. On Monday, their homework would be there, graded, but they wouldn't be there to pick it up. Whatever homework wasn't picked up on Monday was collected by the professor and put out again the subsequent week, along with the freshly graded batch of homework. Slowly over the semester, the pile of uncollected homework grew, and the names of those who weren't attending the lectures became apparent to everyone. On the last day of the class, shortly before handing out the final, the professor let the class know that he had been paying attention to this and told those in attendance that not only was the habit of not picking up graded homework hurting those students because they weren't learning from their mistakes, but it also would harm them in another way. You see, he had made a list of those who hadn't shown an effort in his class, and he then determined that those on the list who enrolled in his supplemental course would be automatically dropped, their places given to those who had made the effort.

Remember that a professor's goal is to teach you the subject matter, not give you a bad grade. Professors want you to succeed, so help them help you.

Another wonderful thing about professors is that they can be essential to your network. They know professionals in your field and have relationships with people who can help launch your career. Professors are also great sounding boards when you need help with a problem in an internship; they are the built-in mentors of the college campus. Creating lifelong relationships and taking the time here to let them get to know you on a personal level can be one of the best decisions you make while in school.

NOTE FROM PROFESSOR HAYS: This couldn't be more true! Networking with your professors matters to your success. Last summer I planned on working on this book, helping coordinate a big event, and researching a project. Because of the way my contract is at Fresno State, I am technically off during the summer. Being who I am, I still check my e-mail, but I mostly inform people to check back with me in August, and we'll solve all of their problems then. Occasionally, of course, I get a frantic student request that needs to be dealt with immediately, and this is where I've got a choice. And, to be quite frank, *who* the request comes from is the most important thing I consider. Is this a request from someone who has made a point of getting engaged in my program and has contributed? Is this someone who only contacts me when they want something? Is this someone I would even recognize if he or she were standing in front of me? I sometimes refer to this as "having skin in the game." I'm not even sure what it exactly means, but it's a cliché that references the fact that if someone puts out effort, I will put out effort, too. If not, I don't feel tremendously obligated to help. You might think that this is harsh, but I'm actually hopeful that you are the same way. Why should *you* care more about somebody else's problem than they do? So, that summer, as with every summer, I received some "urgent" requests. One day I got two, and my responses were very different: One student I helped immediately, even though it was actually a harder fix than the other request. The other request I ignored, because the reason it was last minute was a choice, not based on circumstance, and this student had been very consistent in her inability to have some "skin in the game."

Another way this manifests itself is via internships and job opportunities. When I get an especially interesting internship or job opportunity, I do my best to make a good match. Obviously, the students who have shown the most effort are the ones that come to mind most quickly, and those are the ones who get the leads first. If a student has networked with me, gotten to know me, and also shared what they are most interested in, I am sometimes able to connect them with their dream opportunity. On the day I wrote this paragraph I connected one student with the perfect self-publishing site for a family memoir he is writing, and another with my friend from high school who works in a related business in the city where she wants to move. Both of these students had shown effort in their coursework and in their networking with me, and both of them are very happy as a result.

Now, there will be some professors who are just unapproachable or whom you don't "click" with. Don't panic. Do the best you can to foster a relationship, and sometimes it will grow over time. Sometimes it doesn't, and that's okay as well. You can reach all of your goals without being BFFs with every professor you've ever had. Be strategic and build relationships with the ones you spend the most time with. And it's also okay if one or two of your best professor-student relationships are with people outside of your field. They can be helpful in a number of ways, even if only to offer a different perspective on an idea, a project, a problem, or life itself!

Go Above and Beyond

The next step is to go above and beyond the requirements of the class. If an instructor asks for a project a certain way, expand upon the project and do it even better. Aim to hand in the best version of this project your professor has ever received. When you go the extra mile, your professors see that excitement and willingness to work harder, and, more often than not, you are rewarded for it.

College projects are also a chance to decide what type of worker you are. Are you someone who does the project exactly as specified? Are you easily motivated? Do you ask a lot of questions to clarify that you're doing it right? Do you like to get creative and make the most you can out of every project? Do you love or hate team projects? This can all be invaluable information for you to learn before you enter the workforce, because it helps you identify jobs that suit your work style.

Tip: When you graduate from college, a big learning curve will be not getting graded on your work. Start building up your work ethic while you're still in college by only turning in work you are proud of. Countless interns hand in something adequate and call it finished when they could have spent a little more time on it and produced a great piece of work. In the real world, you want to make sure every project you complete is a sample of your best effort. (A great way to do this is to give yourself wiggle room so you have time to spend on your projects. Read more about this in chapter 7.)

Read More . . . and More Often

I'm going to tell you to do something that you really won't want to do: Buy the books your professor requires for the coursework, and *keep* them. Don't sell them back at the end of the class—the reading material is much more worthwhile than the little cash you'll be given back for it. Similarly, if your professor mentions titles of other recommended works, buy those too.

Now take a quick breath and relax. This doesn't mean you need to read every book cover to cover. I've been in college, and I know how impossible it is to find time to do anything outside of the workload the professors already give you (especially if you're busy doing everything this book is recommending you to do). What I *am* suggesting is that you get your hands on those recommended books and see how they can help you. Reference them when you need to. One of my goals when I graduated from college and got into the "real world" was to have a book for all the different professional situations I might find myself facing. Trying to remember all that information off the top of my head years later wouldn't have been realistic, feasible, or even worth trying to accomplish. What's important to remember is that usually one section of a book can give you all the information you need; you don't need to read the book in its entirety over and over again.

In fact, I'd recommend you use this book the same way. Sitting and reading it cover to cover is wonderful, but be sure to refer back to specific portions or chapters when applicable in your life so that you've got your bases covered. If you're going to a networking event, refer back to the tips in chapter 8 to motivate you. If you're going into an interview, review chapters 2 and 5 to make sure you have your brand straight and your talking points ready. Bookmarking, folding page corners down, and highlighting sections that you can refer to when needed are all great ways to prepare yourself for success.

If you're strapped for cash, keep a running list of the books you want to buy, and after the semester is over you might have some extra cash from selling back some textbooks or from a paying internship. Invest in your career by learning as much as you can from the recommended reading of people much wiser than you. You can also explore buying books from sources other than the student bookstore. There are many online sites that offer steep discounts.

Join Student Associations

And don't just join—immerse yourself! Get an officer position. Love to take notes and organize? Be the secretary. Are you a natural-born leader? Go for president. And if you don't think there is a position that fits your skills, create it. For example, maybe you are a Web wizard with the ability to create a sophisticated blog or website, but your club doesn't have one. Offer to create and manage it in exchange for a webmaster title and spot as an officer. All student associations are run by volunteers, and if you are willing to dig in and do some meaningful work for that organization, you will be not only encouraged but also cherished.

While you won't have time to join every organization that sounds interesting to you, make sure your prioritized extracurricular activities relate to your chosen future profession. Many times these clubs are also affiliated with national organizations, which can offer you even more value. Then, if you have the time and inclination, consider joining a group that is related to a secondary interest that you have. While you might consider this a "just for fun" club, the relationships you form there will also serve as opportunities for networking, making friends, broadening your horizons, and giving your life balance. All good for your ultimate success!

Attend all the meetings of the organizations you join. Each time a student club meets, it is for a purpose. They may have a professional guest speaker, offer tips to help you in your specific field, or sponsor networking events. All of these are great opportunities and what you are paying for with your association dues. Take advantage of everything they are offering you, because you won't get opportunities like this once you graduate.

Then work hard on the tasks the organization has assigned you, to show that you have the work ethic and self-starter attitude that employers love. This will prove to fellow students, professors, and faculty that you are the whole package.

Generally student associations also keep you apprised of job fairs and other great forums or headhunter agencies where you can send your résumé. These are all chances to get your name out there, practice your interviewing skills, and network. Print out hard copies of your résumé and business card, staple them together, and hand them out everywhere and to everyone. (Yes, you need a business card even if you don't have a job. More on this in chapter 8.)

Get Awarded for Being an Outstanding Student

A lot of these student organizations will offer awards that you can work extra hard to earn and then put in your portfolio and on your résumé. Another great way to get awards is through honor societies or fraternities, or from those professors for whom you've gone above and beyond. Research what opportunities are out there, find out what you need to get recognized, and then take the necessary steps to do it.

Scholarships count and can be a double win, because they offer not only recognition but also money to help pay for your schooling. What's even better? Winning a scholarship that is also a competition. We had several of these types of scholarships in my department. One time we were asked to solve a business's problem using what we'd learned in class and then present our ideas to the business owner in exchange for the chance to win cash. First-, second-, and third-place honors were given, and all of us had a wonderful line item on our résumé. This particular kind of award may not be offered to you, but research and go for the scholarships available to you. Winning them shows you're smart, resourceful, and worth the investment a company might want to make in you.

Outside the Classroom: In the Real World

For the career-minded student (like you), getting experience outside of the classroom and off campus is just as important, if not more so, than the experience gleaned inside the classroom. The most successful gain the edge by capitalizing on opportunities. Don't be stuck with a breadth of work that you've only been graded on; get out there and get real-world experience.

This can be a scary proposition. Stepping off campus is hard, and many students learn too late that experience limited to the classroom or university clubs is insufficient for success after graduation. Students who rely solely on campus-bound opportunities tend to be at a huge disadvantage later on. And so in this chapter we identify how to get off campus, win those coveted internships, and get invaluable real-world experience.

One of the best tips I can offer you in this area, as I mentioned earlier, is to use your student status. It really is true that professionals typically love to help students. If a student calls and asks how a professional got his or her job, inquires about a typical day in that profession, or requests mentoring or help, the student is much more likely to receive the help than a college graduate would. After graduation, students are considered to be grown ups, expected to fend for themselves. But during your undergraduate years, you will be offered a huge array of opportunities that will give you a leg up in your later professional life.

Attend Professional Events

Get involved in professional associations early (both those focused on general networking and those related specifically to your field), and your résumé will already be more impressive than the majority. Career success is all about networking, which we will cover in depth later in this book. Going to professional association events as a student shows you're serious about your career trajectory and want to get an early start on it. These events, like on-campus club meetings, always have a purpose; you won't need to attend all of them, but a number will be of interest to you and can help you toward your ultimate career goals. You can earn a great deal of supplemental knowledge from conferences, one-time workshops, and seminars.

These events help you gain real-world experience: You make the connections to get awards, make your real-world experience work for you, and get the hard-to-attain internships.

A Story

A friend of mine took professional events and career fairs very seriously when he was in college. He went to career fairs and submitted his résumé to every single place that he possibly could. And he didn't just attend these events; he did his research and knew exactly which booths he wanted to visit. He made a plan of attack and followed it. He would make a list of all the companies he wanted to talk to, get a map, plot out where to go, and then head to each booth. Prior to going he would look up his top-five companies online so he could be more knowledgeable about what the company did and what he would be able to offer them. Having "mini-interviews" with so many different potential employers can be nerve-wracking; walking into such a crowded space with so many people is overwhelming. But by taking the time to scout out the layout, including reviewing the map of the booths and planning his approach, he gave himself time to calm down. He'd first casually walk by the booths just to see who he'd be speaking with. Then, after stalking his prey (metaphorically, of course), he initiated his plan of attack: He figured out how his personal experience and education could relate to what they were doing, walked up to the booth, and invariably impressed the representative. Remember, there are a lot of students and job seekers there; you need to stand out!

Get Professionally Awarded for Your Award-Worthy Work

You might be thinking garnering professional awards is difficult, but it is actually more feasible than you think. If you're interning and getting professional experience, you deserve to be awarded just as much as any other rookie or recent graduate out there. You'd be surprised by the amount of awards that are given every year in all lines of work, but many students don't have any in their portfolios because they either don't know they are eligible or don't think the honor is attainable. So how do you break away from the norm?

Find out what awards impact your field, even on a small, local scale. Look at the requirements and who usually wins them. Try to speak to past winners (approach them with some of our tips for networking in chapter 8). Decide which awards you think you have a good chance at getting. Then tailor your internship or projects to fit the parameters of the award committee.

An award earned from a professional association *before* you graduate shows that you are much more involved in the field than the average person. Now, if you don't earn a professional award, please don't be disappointed—these awards are not necessary for hire; they're just a great plus! So, while winning such an award isn't always possible or applicable to every student, I nonetheless urge you to seek out information about available awards, determine who you need to talk to, and find out what you need to do to earn them.

A Story

I was able to win an industry award while I was still a student, which I attribute mostly to my network but also to my innovative tendencies. I worked with the regional professional association that was linked to our student association to help us start an on-campus student-operated public relations firm. It got my face and name out there in the industry at a very early age and helped me forge relationships with the members of the group. It also helped that they met in the building where I held an internship, so I would see them all occasionally as they came in for their monthly board meetings. When it came time for them to give a Rookie of the Year award, I was top-of-mind within the group because I had met with them about the success of the student firm. I was the first student to ever receive the award, and I am still so proud to be a recipient. It took being innovative, nurturing my network, saying thank you, and working very hard!

TIP: If you receive awards, are mentioned in publications, and so on, it is a great idea to bring the paper versions (photocopies or certificates) in a professional folder to an interview. Having the folder can be a talking point, and you can show off all that hard work!

Make Your Real-World Work and Coursework Work for You

When you start interning early and often, you will learn certain things in the real world in concert with your learning in the classroom—sometimes even before. But it's the crossover between theoretical in-class learning and on-the-job practical experience that will be of greatest value to you. Have a marketing plan due in class? Offer to do it as a project for a local business as part of an internship project, and you'll get a real-world piece for your portfolio and an A+ grade, and the business will have a stellar plan of attack.

Seek out real-world opportunities to practice what you are doing in class. When you've learned a new technique or theory in class, find a way to put it into professional practice. Find a nonprofit and offer your services. Ask your internship supervisor if you can work on something similar for them. This will reinforce what you've learned in class, help you really understand what you are doing, give you another project or piece for that portfolio, and provide another great real-world reference.

A Story

When a friend of mine started taking his engineering courses, he realized much of what he had done in his internships was applicable to his classes. He made it known to his professor that he had experience in what they were learning about in class, going back to high school; he already had hands-on knowledge about what the professor was teaching. While the professor still had a lot to teach him about methods he had never used before, my friend was able to pick up on much of the material very easily, and much more quickly than other students in the class.

My friend didn't rely solely on internships and work outside of class to start his career: He got involved on campus and in class as well, and telling his professors about his previous experience and working hard in class made him stand out.

Volunteer

Volunteering helps you break free from the crowd because it shows how committed you are to your industry and to increasing your knowledge and skills. Volunteer experience is in a different section on your résumé from your school and professional experience (which we'll cover more in chapter 11 when we put all these topics together), and so you should put just as much effort into this area as you do into your school and work. Volunteering is also the perfect way to start practicing innovation. When you volunteer at an organization, they'll let you wear as many hats as you want and give you as much experience as possible. Go into the organization with an open mind, and brainstorm ways that you could make a real difference. The more innovative you are, the better. People at the organization will take notice, and you'll get great recommendations, new network connections, and maybe even a job with them—because why wouldn't they want to hire you?

Volunteering is also good for your soul. Not worrying about money and doing something for sheer enjoyment is priceless. So get out into your community and volunteer your time and talents!

A Story

When I was in college I took deaf studies classes to earn a minor in American Sign Language. While it had nothing to do with my major, I loved learning the language, and the extra work was worth it to me. Part of one of the courses was volunteering at the local deaf community center. I went in to complete my hours, and they asked me to file some paperwork and do some other administrative tasks. I started paying attention to what was going on at the center and learned that there was a large event coming up. I asked how they were getting awareness out about their event and if they needed any help. It turned out that they had no plan and were excited to have my help as a public relations student. Rather than spending the rest of my hours buried in paperwork like my peers, I spent it writing press releases, media alerts, and e-mails to media members that I knew to help the center get some attention. Thanks to my hours, the center had TV crews at their event for the first time as well as a great turnout of participants. Not only were the folks at the center happy, but I also had more great pieces for my portfolio. And a year later they e-mailed asking for my help again, this time for pay. Bottom line: Pay attention, be innovative, and the rewards will come.

Get Internships

This message is simple but more powerful than just about anything else we tell you in this book. Get internships. Need me to tell you again? *Get internships*—as early and often as possible. And don't worry about pay (at first). Every internship will lead to bigger and better opportunities. Realize that you will most likely have to do an unpaid internship or project at some point in your early career, and believe me, it is *much* better to be unpaid when you are in school and have financial aid or your parents to help support you. After you put in those hard-working hours at the unpaid or low-paying companies, move on to companies that see your breadth of work and are willing and able to pay you what you deserve (or at least close).

> TIP TO GETTING INTERNSHIPS: Make yourself stand out.

Use Your Network

We'll talk more about this in chapter 8, but let everyone know that you are looking and able to take on opportunities. These professors to whom you've been showing initiative are great resources for possible on- and off-campus opportunities. Other students, especially older ones, may be leaving internships and can recommend you directly to their employers. This is a best-case scenario that worked for me.

A Story

I was about to leave an internship and wasn't completely sure what to do next. Luckily, I still had a great relationship with Professor Hays, and she told me that another student who had an internship one step up from what I was doing would be graduating that year. I reached out to that student, learned more about what she did, and was excited for the chance to move up in the world. After meeting with the student and Professor Hays, they both recommended me for the position, and it was an easy transition into my next phase of internships on the road to my dream career.

If you have a family member, neighbor, or friend in your industry, see if they have any opportunities where you could help out. Remember, always approach them offering help, not asking for them to do something for you. If you start out offering your services for free, they'll definitely throw projects at you, or let you observe, and you can start gaining real-world experience right away.

Be Prepared at All Times

Be prepared for your next career step! Even if you aren't actively look-ing for a new internship or job, it is always good to be prepared for the next big thing. Continue to maintain the brand you created in chapter 2, create talking points around that brand, and keep your résumé updated with recent accomplishments. Always think about how your services could help those around you, and be ready to offer them when an opportunity arises.

This also means being prepared when going into an interview. Don't just show up ready to talk about yourself. Know the business you are applying for inside and out. Study recent press releases and who their clients, supporters, vendors, or partners are. Look at their company history. While using online sources is the obvious place to begin this type of research, actual humans are great sources as well. Former interns, people who work in the department you want to work in, and anyone else who has worked with that organization are all good places to start.

TIP: Find any connections you have to their brand, and make sure they hear about it. Relate things their company is doing to what you are learning in class or in a current internship. And then create and bring a set of questions.

Get a general understanding of what you will be doing for the company, and if something doesn't make sense, ask for clarification. This shows them that you are interested and that you are knowledgeable about both their company and your role. While it may seem counterintuitive, asking more questions can generally make you look smarter. At the very least, it shows your thorough interest in their company, as well as your excellent ability to conduct research. Be sure to include a few questions that have to do with overall organization strategy: mission statement, organization chart, association with parent company (if there is one), partner organizations, and so forth. Showing that you value information about the big picture of the company will help your interviewer believe that you know how important that big picture is, even if you won't be dealing with it directly.

Tip: I cannot stress enough the importance of researching companies you are interested in and keeping your résumé up to date. Before going into an interview, research who will be interviewing you in order to know what they do for the company and what they are specifically looking for in a candidate. Find out how you would fit in their company. Then, in the interview, focus on these points, and talk about yourself in a positive manner. Remember, luck is when opportunity meets preparedness. So be prepared!

Brag

This is a tough directive for most. In this day and age, and especially for girls, we are taught that it is rude to talk about yourself too much. But the key here is to brag without letting people realizing that you're doing it: by making your résumé a story.

For example, if someone asks you, "What do you do?" don't say, "I've built fifteen bridges, and I'm great at it—the best bridge builder there ever was." Instead, try weaving your résumé points into a story: "I was one of those kids who never wanted to share my LEGOs. I was constantly building everything I could, and as I got older becoming a bridge builder just made sense. Since then I've been fortunate enough to build fifteen bridges that I'm very proud of, one of which won an award for . . ."

Presenting your strengths as a narrative not only shifts the attention off of you and onto your résumé points but also adds personal interest and can even incorporate your sense of humor and what makes you different from all of the other candidates being interviewed.

Always have different bragging points in the back of your mind. Constantly be conscious of what you've done recently that people will find interesting and impressive. Then flesh out on paper how to speak about each point without coming across as rude (or conceited). Make these points part of your story and your charm. Then recite the story back to yourself, and you'll be ready to share with others when *the right situation arrives*.

Don't assume everyone wants to hear everything about you all the time, no matter how great you are. Wait until someone asks you a question or until a conversation lends itself to your sharing about relevant accomplishments. If you start in about yourself without any prompting, you can turn people off what you're saying, no matter how great it is. So pay attention to the conversation around you, and *listen*. When the right time comes, jump on it, and get your brag on.

Have Great Manners

Always say thank you. Manners go a very long way in the interviewing process and can help you stand out from the crowd. When you finish interviews, say thank you. Then e-mail a thank you message. Then send a follow-up thank you note. (You will notice that we discuss thank yous a lot in this book, for good reason. They are important and go a long way toward helping you accomplish your goals.)

A Story

When Megan interviewed for a coveted and well-paid internship at a nonprofit center on campus, she knew the competition was fierce. She researched the position and the person who was going to interview her, and she talked to the last two interns who had held that position for advice. She consulted with her professors and felt really good after the initial interview. True to her nature (and her upbringing), she sent a hand-written thank you note after the interview. The internship supervisor was so pleased (and surprised) that she texted a picture of the thank you card to Megan's professor with a note that read, "Yes, she's the one." Lesson confirmed.

Here are some other behaviors that showcase your great manners:

- Punctuality.

- Open and hold doors open for others (whether you are male or female).

- Allow others to enter rooms before you.

- Have a firm handshake.

- Admire business cards—no matter what they look like—and always give one in return.

- Stay to the right on sidewalks and stairwells.

- Use eye contact (or look at their nose, like when you are giving a presentation).

- Wait to eat until everyone at your table has been served.

- When you sit to eat, remember your BMW (no, not the car)—Bread is on the left, Meal in the middle, and Water/Wine on the right.

- Only have at most one alcoholic drink at work events (it's better for your health and your image).

- Place your phone (and other tech devices) out of sight when you are spending time with others.

- Focus on people at events and parties (not food).

- And, of course, say "please" when you ask for something, just as often as you say "thank you."

When you are polite, punctual, and respectful and you follow up, you stand out. Always thank the interviewer for their time, but do not be pushy. Don't call or e-mail them constantly, but make your presence known—let them know that you are interested and appreciative so you can get that edge you need.

If any of this seems overwhelming, or you think you'd like more tips, take an etiquette class. You'll learn way more than you think, and it's applicable to business events as well as impressing your friends and family at events. It's always fun to have etiquette information to share, and people will think you're more knowledgeable and know that you care about your brand.

Interview Tips

Always be on time to an interview—and on time means a little early! (Remember chapter 2.) Give yourself plenty of time to get there, especially if you don't know where you are going or if there is a chance of traffic. Once you get there, scope the place out. Figure out which office you need to go to and how long you have left before your interview. (Remember that you don't want to be too early; that's impolite too.) If you're early enough, grab a cup of coffee or munch on a nonmessy snack to give yourself an energy boost.

Before you walk into the interview, take a minute to check yourself in a mirror. Realign that skirt, straighten that tie, and make sure your hair is in place and that your shirt is tucked in properly. Oh, and do you have anything stuck in your teeth? Any of these things can be a huge distraction from your glowing résumé, impressive demeanor, and warm smile. Make sure you maintain eye contact, are pleasant, and maintain good posture. Keep your responses concise; always leave the interviewer wanting more information, and aim to answer each question in a few sentences. A great way to practice this is by role-playing beforehand with a friend. Set up a practice interview, and have your helper ask you questions so you can rehearse answers, learning how to ad-lib when needed as your helper asks unplanned questions. This will obviously improve your interview skills, and it will also boost your confidence. Confidence in an interview is an amazing asset. Think back to when you met someone for the first time: Were they nervous? Did they avoid eye contact and mumble? Did that impress you? I'm thinking that answer is *no*. These behaviors won't impress your interviewer either.

All of those things your parents and teachers told you (repeatedly) while you were growing up will make you look more professional and ready to take on the world. And while many of these recommendations are small details, they make a big difference to the person reviewing your résumé and make you look that much more eager and ready to start your career.

A Story

I personally believe in internships because they were key to my early career start. One of my first internships was unpaid with my department's alumni board. I told my professor on the board that I was actually a really good writer, and within a week she set up an interview for me with a nonprofit entrepreneurship center. I went from no money to a large stipend per semester—a huge step up. From that internship I was able to make contacts to start my own business and moved on to my first real-world job while still in my third year of college. If I hadn't been prepared and willing to brag about myself to my network, I would have stayed at the unpaid gig for much longer. And, of course, I said thank you to my professor! (P.S. The professor I bragged to back then is the same Betsy Hays coauthoring this book years later—another example of how the principles in this book really work.)

How to Be a Good Intern

When in Doubt, Ask!

Don't assume you know everything, and don't assume that your manager expects you to know everything. If you're unsure about something, ask for help and find out the answer from the correct person. Your manager can help you react and respond to situations that make you feel uncomfortable or distressed. Remember that he or she has been where you are and knows many things learned only through experience. While you are a student you can also ask your professors, mentors, or peers for advice. Your network is also a great resource here. But if your question is specific to your position or company, and especially if you are dealing with sensitive information, please reach out to your manager. Their job is to help you succeed!

TIP: If possible, try to group questions for the same person. For example, if you've just started your job, keep a running list of questions as you get acquainted with your responsibilities. Then, when your manager is available and open to speak with you, ask all of your questions at the same time. This will show organized thought and respect for your manager's time.

Be Responsible

Even though you are a student, you don't want some of the possible negative stereotypes about students to ring true about you (i.e., not caring, being irresponsible, etc.). Whether you are paid or not, you've made a commitment to that organization, and they deserve your full effort. Plus, the reputation and opinion of whoever recommended you for the internship is on the line. If you don't believe you can give your full effort to a company, don't take on the internship, and wait until you can. Always be on time, and show up ready to work. You are a part of their team, and, remember, there is no *I* in *team*.

Call When You Will Be Late or Absent

Doing so also falls under "being responsible." Don't waste other people's time or leave them wondering what to do or where you are. Obviously, try your best to never be late or absent, but let your manager know when you will be, giving them as much notice as possible. Help the team make arrangements for your absence, if necessary, so no one is left confused.

TIP: If you are absent for more than a day, create an automatic response e-mail in which you explain that you will be out of the office, those whom people can contact if they need immediate assistance, and when you will return. When you return from your absence, respond to all e-mail and messages in a timely manner, and thank people for their patience. And make sure you turn the automatic response off!

Respect Your Company's Privacy

Always be mindful of which information is private, especially if your company has you sign any nondisclosure agreements or privacy-related documents. If you have access to confidential information about your company or anyone your company works with, be sure to treat that information with respect. If you are reporting about your company for a class, or using some of the work toward a class project, be sure to remove that sensitive information or use pseudonyms when referring to people you work with or clients.

Show Respect, Period

Remember that you have been given a great opportunity by the company that hired you. Working as an intern is a privilege, and the organization is investing in you just as much as you are working for them. They are giving you valuable resources and the opportunity to learn in your industry, so thank them by being a respectful employee. Don't complain when you are given a dull task (which you will most likely get at least once as an intern, unless you are *extremely* lucky); instead, take it on with a smile, and remember that they are helping you on your career path just as much as, if not more than, you are helping them in their operation. Follow all rules of the organization, and be polite to everyone in the office.

Be Appropriate

Just as you protect your brand outside of the workplace, protect it in the office. Be appropriate in the office, following the guidelines set forth by your company. Dress appropriately, treat others with courtesy and kindness, and use formal names unless otherwise noted. Watch your language in the workplace, and be mindful that your words are hard to put back in your mouth. Set a positive example of what motivated students are really like, and only do or say what needs to be done or said to build your brand. Be friendly, and you will earn more fans in the office.

A Story

It seems a bit silly now, but I didn't call Professor Hays by her first name until my senior year, and even then it was tough. She was my professor, my boss for a while, and then one of my best friends and mentors. Then I went with her to take her dog, Max, to the animal hospital for a checkup. Somehow he got loose from his leash, and I had to tackle him to keep him from running away. After that I felt we were finally close enough that I could call her Betsy. (I mean, I did get grass stains on my jeans trying to save her dog!) I wanted to show as much respect as possible, which I attribute to my conservative upbringing. But even if you weren't raised to use formal titles, get in the practice now. Always call people Professor, Mister, Miss, or Missus Lastname. Always. Until they tell you to call them something else.

Be Flexible

Like I mentioned earlier, you may be given less-than-exciting tasks as an intern. Many companies hire interns for the sole purpose of getting a list of things done they just don't have time to do. This isn't an insult to you; it's just that they don't know what you can handle, yet. When you start your internship, take on every responsibility given to you, and do it above and beyond requirement and expectation. Prove to those you work for that you can handle all of the responsibility they've given you and more. Then they'll be more open to giving you greater responsibility and tasks you enjoy.

A Story

My husband, David, studied civil engineering in college, but he knew as early as high school that it was the career path for him. His neighbor worked as a city foreman for a construction crew and told David about a summer-internship program he was running for students. Even though he know that the job would be pretty much all manual labor, David decided to go for it anyway because it was related to the field of engineering he was interested in, it gave him hands-on experience, and he would be paid well. What he didn't expect, however, was the amount of knowledge and affirmation of his professional choices he would receive from the job. It gave David an inside look at what the field was actually like, and he was able to see from a "bottom of the ladder" standpoint what he was striving for in the long run. He could personally see the position three levels above himself and knew that was what he was working so hard to achieve.

David soaked up all the knowledge he could in that first internship, and when it came time to get college internships his experience paid off. He believes that one reason his first college internship wanted him was because he had experience in the public sector. He was working on his degree, so they knew he was well educated, but they also knew that he had working knowledge of the responsibilities and that he would adjust quickly—definitely more quickly than other applicants—to how the public sector worked.

In many companies, you may not be able to predict the level of activity or intensity. Be flexible to changing situations and responsibilities. Reach out to help anyone else you can when they need it, and try to help the company run smoothly overall. Being an intern means that you can wear many hats and help as many others as possible. Get your hands dirty, and you'll come out of the position knowing much more than you ever intended to learn.

A Story

My first corporate internship was part of a huge program consisting of about one hundred interns. I was assigned to a department in the large company, and they had a list of all the items they wanted me to work on for the summer. I finished the list that was supposed to last me all summer in about three weeks, with many more weeks to go. I told my manager, who had no idea what else to give me. So I offered my help to other departments to assist their interns if needed. (Sadly, all the other departments refused my help because they were worried they wouldn't have enough for both their interns and me.) In my boredom, I shadowed some other workers, conducted informational interviews, helped with presentations and projects, took the company's Microsoft Office courses, volunteered for small projects around the office, updated my social networks, and read books. I'll never forget one employee (probably someone who has yet to get promoted) telling me that I shouldn't work so quickly, because then my only reward would be getting more work to do. Needless to say, I didn't go back to intern at this company and decided that this particular corporate pace wasn't what I was looking for. But the point is that I was flexible and made work for myself, even when they didn't have any for me. And the knowledge that I didn't want to work in the corporate arena, together with some fantastic informational interviews, great work experience, and new friends, was more than worth my time that summer. Plus, I got paid!

NOTE: Not all corporations, firms, start-ups, or nonprofits will work at the same pace. Try interning at a few different companies in each sector to really get a feel for which pace you prefer.

Be Smart

When working at any company, use your brain. Know what is right and wrong. For example, never show up to work under the influence of drugs or alcohol, never loan money to (or take money from) clients whom you work with, never drive clients around in your personal car, never make promises that you can't keep, and never behave in a way that can be perceived as sexual or discriminatory. Don't enter into romantic or sexual relationships with people you work with, and don't start business relationships with clients outside of your company's scope. And if you ever feel that you or your rights are violated, report it right away. Follow up, and make sure that person or people are held accountable. No one in your company ought to expect any less, and in fact they will respect you more for your ability to handle these issues as an adult.

Another Story about David

David attributes his ability to land a full-time job before graduation to sending his résumé everywhere possible. He talked to headhunting firms, recruiting firms, and basically anyone who would talk to him. Ultimately, it was a combination of his on- and off-campus efforts that led him to his dream job. One of the many headhunter agencies he gave his résumé to included his résumé in an e-mail to a city listing students looking for employment and internships. David's résumé stood out because he already had hands-on experience as well as related coursework. He was a double win because he had the education and the school experience to prove he was smart enough to do the job as well as the real-world experience to show he had the understanding of practical application. As a result, David won a successful interview with a city he didn't even know existed for a job opening he hadn't even known was posted!

Be Innovative

While you are an intern, make sure your employers notice you and the value you bring to the company. We have covered a few ways that you can stand out, but one of my long-time friends, Anne, has a great story about innovation in internships.

A Story

Anne held an internship at MTV in the human-resources department while she was still in college, but her boss was extremely busy and didn't give any of the interns much direction. Anne took her internship into her own hands and set out to make a difference in the department. She contacted several schools in the Los Angeles area and talked to their career center coordinators, letting them know about the internship program and encouraging them to apply for upcoming semesters. Anne's initiative resulted in a few of the schools asking her to come speak to their students and recruit. Anne also helped improve MTV's intern orientation and created a Facebook group for each semester's set of interns so they could all learn from each other's experiences. At the end of the internship Anne's boss was so impressed that she asked to keep Anne on for another semester and then went above and beyond in helping Anne with her job search.

Now, if you've done all of this right, you will walk into your interviews completely prepared with both in-class and real-world work that shines. You'll also have several academic and practicing professionals' referrals to help convince your dream company that you are the best candidate for the job you want. And even better? You might have a few awards to take with you that will push your résumé to the top of the pile.

Cheat Sheet

- Immerse yourself inside the classroom and on campus.
  - Know your professor.
  - Go above and beyond.
  - Read more . . . and more often.
  - Join student associations.
  - Get awarded for your student work.

- Immerse yourself outside the classroom in the real world.
  - Attend professional events.
  - Get awarded.
  - Make your real-world work and coursework work for you.

- ○ Volunteer.
- ○ Get internships.

- How to get an internship?
  - ○ Use your network.
  - ○ Be prepared to take advantage of opportunities at all times.
  - ○ Brag.
  - ○ Have great manners.
  - ○ Give a great interview.
  - ○ Add value as an intern.
  - ○ When in doubt, ask.
  - ○ Be responsible.
  - ○ Call when you will be late or absent.
  - ○ Respect your company's privacy.
  - ○ Be respectful, period.
  - ○ Be appropriate.
  - ○ Be flexible.
  - ○ Be smart.

CHAPTER FOUR
EMPLOY THE MAGIC OF 75/25
Professor Hays

The 75/25 rule is one that you can use in all areas of your life—personal and professional. What's great about this rule is that the more you use it, the happier and more successful you will be. You'll be less stressed, more productive, and probably in better physical shape. You will also accomplish all of your goals faster and with more precision. Sound appealing? I thought so!

You employ the magic of the 75/25 rule by spending 75 percent of your time thinking and 25 percent of your time doing. Sounds simple, right? You are probably already noticing that the ideas in this book are deceptively simple. Our ideas are easy to understand, and they all make sense. The challenge is in the implementation. Succeeding at life is not complicated, but there is a catch: You have to put in the work and stay focused—the two fundamental things that most people don't do regularly. You also have to put in the *right* work, which is what this rule allows you to do. If you regularly put in the right work and are diligently focused, you'll get what you want out of life.

So let's get into this a little deeper. First of all, just for fun, think of the people in your life who employ the opposite of this rule. They think 25 percent of the time and do 75 percent of the time. Maybe you are even this type of person. (Don't worry—we will cure you in this chapter!) These are the people who always run around like the proverbial chickens with their heads cut off. And for some reason they are always flailing their arms. They also are constantly stressed, late, overwhelmed, and occasionally tough to spend time with, *as their anxiety can rub off on you if you are not careful.* When we act first and think later, we cause a myriad of problems including do-overs, mistakes, and embarrassment. I don't know about you, but that seems like a good list to avoid.

To make the 75/25 idea even more appealing, consider that when you think more, you actually have to do less. You'll also discover that some things aren't necessary or worth doing. You'll also redo things less frequently. Think of how many times you've had to do something over because you didn't think it through first. Bet this has happened to you more than once, like with all of us. Well, it's time to inch the number of those instances to closer to zero. And, through thinking more and doing less, you'll figure out ways to do things better, faster, and more efficiently.

Slow Down

The reason why most people employ the opposite of the 75/25 rule is their inability to slow down. The world moves quickly, and the pace of life can be fast and furious. It is easy to get caught up in this pace, but if you allow yourself to do so, you are setting yourself up to be less successful. My late father, whom I loved so dearly, was an extremely wise man who was very proud of his daughter (me). But there was one thing about me that frustrated him—the fact that I had "issues" with slowing down. For years, it drove me crazy that he was always telling me to slow down, and, in typical teenage-and-young-adult-rebellion fashion, it only made me go faster. It has only been in the years since I started teaching this rule that I understand the importance of his two simple words: slow down.

If you are going to spend 75 percent of your time thinking and 25 percent of your time doing, you are going to have to slow down. You are going to have to take deep breaths, and you are going to have to take them regularly. You need to spend parts of every day, every week, and every month unplugged and disconnected from the rest of the world. This is when you'll figure out what the "right" work is that you need to put in for your life to become what you want it to be, and this is what will keep you focused. These are the two keys to your success.

What Should You Think About?

For starters, you need to spend time on the big picture of your life—what your big goals are and where you want to be headed. The first time you do this will take the most time, and after that you'll need to spend shorter amounts of time fine-tuning.

So, think about the big picture of your life right now: Identify the roles that you have—student, employee, intern, sister or brother, friend, boyfriend or girlfriend, club officer, and so forth. Make a list. Then jot down the areas of your life that are important to you. This could include health, work, school, internship, painting, cooking, reading, video games, family, your blog—whatever. This is a personal list.

Then think about the big picture of your life in general: What do you want to accomplish? What are your short- and long-term goals? Jot these down as well.

After you have this probably overwhelming look at the big picture of your life, both now and toward the future, prioritize it. It's likely a big list, and it's probably unrealistic to focus on it all right now, so make decisions about what areas are most important *right now* (this week, month, semester/quarter).

This is where you will become aware of my belief that you can absolutely have *everything* you want in life. The catch is that you can't have it all at once. There will be things that have to wait until later, until a different time in your life. If it is important to you, you'll figure out how to get it done. It just may have to wait, and this is okay. Make a list of these things, and save the list for your life/time review sessions (which we'll discuss later in this chapter).

If you are having trouble choosing your priorities, here are two questions to help you. The first one is as follows: "What is the legacy you want to leave behind?" I am very hopeful that you have decades and decades before anyone talks about your legacy, but if you are going to have one, you may want to get started. Normally, a legacy takes a lifetime to achieve. The second question is this: "If someone looked at how you spend your time, would they know what your priorities are?" If not, you might want to adjust things.

Once you have your Priorities Right Now list, identify the tasks with the most value in those areas. These tasks should have a high return on investment (ROI), meaning that for the time and energy you spend you will receive something of significant value. These are the things you will want to do first each day, before things get away from you. Let me repeat: Do the things that advance your life first, and then do the rest. By focusing on your high-value tasks, you'll spend less time on the things that can suck the minutes and hours and energy out of your day that don't really give you much in return. This will take discipline, but, again, as discussed above, spending time on the right things and staying focused are the two keys to success. (As you go through this book, we will give you many things to include on your list of tasks that offer the most value for your pending dream career.)

Having these things in mind each day will help you say both yes or no more confidently and with more commitment. You will be able to assess each opportunity based on your priorities and figure out very quickly whether or not it's a good one for *you*. No one likes a flake, and you will be less flaky if you only say yes to the opportunities that help you make your life how you want it to be.

The Compounding Effect

The compounding effect is one of the most wonderful things in the entire world. You probably are familiar with the idea as it relates to money and interest, but it doesn't just work its magic there. The compounding effect can get you just about anything you want. The key: work toward each of your goals in small increments on most days. Want to write a book? Write for a period of time each day. Want to lose weight? Exercise most days. Want to have amazing abdominal muscles? Work on your abs most days. Want to read a book a week? Read some every night before you go to sleep.

Life success is not about perfection; it's about consistency. All of the little things you spend time on each day add up to big results. Many of us waste time waiting for large chunks of time to magically appear in our day in order to get our big projects done, and this just doesn't happen. It's the few minutes a day on the things that are important that get the jobs done. Start employing the compounding effect today. Again, you'll have to make choices (maybe less TV or social media), but it will be worth it!

Carve Out Time to Think

You might be tempted to skip this section, as your knee-jerk reaction to reading this heading might have been "Seriously? I don't have time to think!" This is a common reaction, but stick with me for a bit, and I'll help you find the time. It's not as hard as you think.

To employ the magic of the 75/25 rule to its fullest extent, you'll want to carve out time to think each day, each week, and each month.

Daily (or close to daily), spend some time thinking about something. This is easily done on your drive(s) to work or school, or maybe during your exercise time. Instead of letting your mind just wander, give it an assignment. I walk my dog almost every day, and several times a week I choose what to brainstorm about prior to starting on our walk. This could be very focused thinking (like how to approach a particular lecture or class assignment) or broader thinking (like how I could eat healthier). Every time, I have some great ideas at the end of my walk. Some people like to just type on a blank computer screen, or sit and jot ideas in a notebook. If you can find time to do either or both of these, terrific!

Whenever you decide to have some thinking time, it is important to unplug and disconnect from all distractions. You'll get more thinking done in less time, and you'll actually accomplish your thinking goals. So, turn off all electronic devices, and just be alone with your thoughts. You'll probably think of e-mails or texts to send during this thinking process, but don't do them until your allotted thinking time is over. Make notes, and send them later. Try as best you can to stay focused.

I realize that some days are so full of activities that you can't spend time thinking, but try as best you can to do it as many days as you can.

Carve Out Time to Do Life/Time Reviews

Weekly, set aside some time (again, walking or driving time works for this as well), and review your week. How did it go? What went well? What didn't? Are you making progress toward your Priorities Right Now? Are you taking advantage of the compounding effect? Make some mental and physical notes regarding how next week can be even better.

Monthly, do the same thing, but use a little more effort. Make sure your priorities are the same and that you are aligning your time with them the way *you* want to.

Think Before You Start Anything

When you have a new project, take the time at the beginning to think it through. How much time do you need to complete it? What resources do you need? Do you need help from others? What time of day is best for working on this project? Anticipate problems, anticipate reactions, and ask lots of questions. Really work through things as best you can before you get started.

Then take all of this information and make a time line, plan, or project map—whichever works best for you. If this project has a deadline, note it, and, using the information above, work backward from there to give yourself ample time to get it done (paying careful attention to whether or not you need others' help).

Remember the old carpenter's adage—"measure twice, cut once." This is one of my favorite sayings, as it saves so much grief and wasted time.

Write It Down

Once you've done some beautiful thinking, make sure you capture it. Don't waste those helpful thoughts! Have a notebook with you at all times (even if you typically make notes on your Smartphone or other electronic device). In fact, buy several notebooks, and put one by your bed (for those wonderful 3 A.M. thoughts), put one in your purse or backpack, one in your car, one in your utensil drawer in the kitchen, and so forth.

Have a way to organize your thoughts. Checklists, to-do lists (electronic or hard copy), and calendars are all good tools. There are many great books and blogs about how to get organized and wonderful apps that you can utilize, so use them! My personal favorite is Evernote (available both online and in an app), and I have also successfully used Remember the Milk as well.

Here are some other tips:

- Spend time at the end of each week organizing the next week, confirming all of your meetings and appointments, and scheduling time for those things that are important to you. This way you can hit the ground running on Monday rather than losing a day to getting your act together.

- Spend time at the end of each day organizing for the next.

- Start each day with a priority to-do list. These are the few things that must be done that day. Do these first.

- Remember the compounding effect. Small and regular steps toward all goals are how you actually accomplish things.

- Have a place to capture thoughts about all current and future projects. You don't want to waste your beautiful thinking or, worse, have to think about the same thing or solve the same problem twice.

- Don't rely on your memory for anything. Use your brain for new and creative thinking, not remembering. Let your lists take care of the remembering.

The Creativity Bonus

Spending more time thinking will also get you one of life's best bonuses—creativity. It is virtually impossible to be creative when you spend 25 percent of your time thinking and 75 percent of your time doing. Our brains need time to do their best work.

One important note about creativity—it can level any playing field. A lot of people think that it's the folks with the most money that always win, but it isn't—it's the people who are most creative. And the best part of that truth? Creativity is *free*! There is no socioeconomic status associated with being creative. The option is open to us all. The biggest checkbook and the deepest pockets will fail if the thinking is weak.

To tie this back in to the 75/25 rule, you are able to be creative when you allow yourself time to think. When you slow down and ponder, you can have some wonderful, amazing ideas.

Choose Accuracy over Speed

In this era of information overload and lightning-fast Internet and wire-less this and wired that, it is easy to get caught in the (pardon the pun) speed trap. It is so easy these days to be fast! And anyone can be fast, so being fast is no longer special like it used to be.

Accuracy, on the other hand, is still special, and becoming increasingly rare because of this increased pressure to be first and to be fastest. By slowing down and using the 75/25 rule, you can rework your personal culture to choose accuracy over speed. Again, this allows you to make fewer mistakes, redo less, do less in general, and make your life a whole lot easier.

Some tips:

- Reread your e-mails before hitting send.

- Reread your texts before you hit that button on your phone.

- Let drafts sit for a while before you edit them. And then edit them. And then let them sit some more. And then edit them again.

- Proofread on hard copy only (not on the screen), and read aloud when you proof.

- Have an additional pair of eyes look at critical items prior to distribution.

- Think about the voicemail you will leave before you dial.

Slow it down a bit, double-check things, and you'll establish a reputation for always getting things right the first time, something that will make you stand out in the best possible way. Mistakes happen, and that's fine, but if you are constantly resending e-mails and documents with a subject line that says "corrected version," you need to take this advice to heart.

A Story

One of my students recently placed an ad on Craigslist looking for a cartoonist for an event we were having. In his quest for speed, he left out a digit in his phone number. Several dozen calls around campus later, someone finally connected me to this Craigslist ad, and we were able to make the correction and book the cartoonist. A lot of time was wasted, and a lot of people now knew about the mistake. This was, of course, embarrassing for all involved, and also unproductive. (Two things to avoid, for sure!) I still keep in touch with this student, and we laugh about this now, but he also notes that he has never made this mistake since and spends much more time double-checking things before they go out.

Choose accuracy over speed every time. Your mistakes are remembered far longer than how quickly someone received the information.

Kill the Procrastination Bug

Ah, procrastination. It's an ailment that plagues all of us at one time or another, but there are some sure-fire remedies if you want them. Read on if you could use a little help killing the procrastination bug.

Get Control of E-mail

One of the most notorious time suckers is e-mail. If you don't have issues with e-mail, you may skip this section. But if you are like just about everyone else on the planet, you need to read this and live it.

But first a disclaimer: No one on the planet was happier about getting e-mail on their phone than I. It was a game-changer, a life-changer, and a wonderful gift that allows me to live a much more interesting and mobile life. That said, I also am extremely aware of the dangers of constantly being in touch with your inbox.

If you want to get your e-mail under control, and stop it from aiding in your procrastination and keeping you from your Priorities Right Now lists, here are some helpful hints:

1. Turn off automatic notifications on all of your devices. Make it so you have to go into e-mail in order to see if there is anything new in your inbox. Just like you decide when to go to your actual physical mailbox, *you* decide when to visit your virtual

inbox, not the other way around. E-mail should work *for* you. You should not be at its beck and call.

2. Select specific times each day to check e-mail. Perhaps morning and afternoon will work, or maybe morning, early afternoon, and evening—whenever works best for you. Choose times when you can actually sit down at your computer and process your e-mail. If you must check e-mail from your phone, do so infrequently and only when necessary, and only when you can actually spend time processing some of it. Also, consider not checking e-mail on most of the weekend, and perhaps spend an hour or so on Sunday processing so you can hit the ground running on Monday morning.

3. When you do check e-mail, process it to the finish. This means answer it, file it, delete it, or put it on your to-do list for later. Play around and develop a system that works for you. E-mail folders are one of the greatest gifts we have in the modern era. Below I've listed the e-mail folders that I use to process my e-mails each time I sit down to work on e-mail. Again, you may want to do something differently, which is fine, but do something with your e-mail so your inbox is constantly empty at the end of your e-mail processing sessions. Notice many of them start with "A," so they live at the top of my e-mail folder list and I can access them quickly.
   a. Action Tomorrow (urgent things that I can't answer quickly during my e-mail processing session)
   b. Action Pending (things that I am waiting to hear back from others about and don't want to fall through the cracks)
   c. Action This Week (things that need to get done this week, but are not urgent, and I can't answer quickly during my e-mail-processing session)
   d. Action Next Week (things that can wait)
   e. Action to Read This Week (self-explanatory)
   f. Action to Read Next Week (things that I read whenever, or if ever, but I can't bring myself to delete them)
   g. A folder for each course I teach and project that I am working on, where I file things that I might need to refer to later

for those projects, but these e-mails do not need action or a response.

4. Use your e-mail folders to get things done. When you sit down to work, don't start with your inbox. Start with wherever you put your urgent e-mails, work on those, get them done, and then process your inbox until you are done. Things won't fall through the cracks, and you'll always be on top of things. And your inbox will be empty often, which is a very wonderful thing for your brain's happiness.

Establish Limits for Social Media

Just like e-mail can be a time sucker, so can social media. Again, a disclaimer: I love social media, I teach social media, and people pay me to teach them how to use social media. So this is not an anti-Facebook rant. This is a "how to put social media in its place in your life" rant.

Just like with your e-mail, change your notification settings so you have to go in to see if you have any new messages. And then pick a few times a day to engage in social media. Frequency is up to you, but frequency should not be "anytime you are bored" or "all day." You'll probably want to engage in social media more frequently than you process e-mail, because you can get in and out more quickly, but you should probably not be on Facebook, Twitter, or whatever more than twice in the morning, twice in the afternoon, and once in the evening. This plan will keep you responsive but also let everyone know that you do have a life. You don't want to be known as the person who is always on Facebook or Twitter.

Remember, everything you do has an opportunity cost. You might recall this notion from economics. When you are engaging in social media, you are not doing something else that might be more valuable for your life. So engage, but be strategic. Get in, engage, post, read, like, retweet, share, and so on, and then get out until the next time.

Set Up Your Physical Spaces

Never underestimate the importance of setting up your physical spaces and what this means for potential success. Having what you need where you need it is essential for the busy student who is going to reach his or her goals. This is extremely closely tied to our 75/25 rule, as setting up your physical spaces requires thinking and planning and the more thinking you do the more time you will save, freeing you up for your Priorities Right Now list and making your life as amazing as it can be.

Setting up your physical spaces can also help you kill the procrastination bug, as running unnecessary errands is a sure-fire way to procrastinate—something I'm sure you are already aware of.

Think of the physical spaces you need to live your life—your desk, your car, your kitchen, your apartment or house, and so forth. What do you need to have in each of these places in order to do what you need to do?

- *Desk.* What supplies do you need? Usually everyone needs printer cartridges, paper, pens, staples, paper clips, and so on, but your list may be different. Make this list, buy the things on it, and keep track of when you are running low so you can buy these things again before you run out.

- *Car.* Do you need to put your gym clothes in there? Do you have enough gas to get to where you need to go tomorrow? Are there other things you need for errands or other tasks that should be placed by the front door so that you don't forget them? Set up a system for having what you need to complete your day ready to go before you leave the house. Most of us benefit from doing this the night before, as mornings tend to be harried.

- *Kitchen.* Do you have what you need to prepare food for the week? Make menus, make grocery lists, and only go shopping once a week. Doing this saves time and money and will probably enable you to eat healthier and less expensively. Each night look at the menu plan for the next day, and do any prep needed (i.e., defrosting or chopping or putting the crock pot on the counter so you have a visual reminder of putting something in it in the morning). Set up the coffee the night before to help your mornings be less crazy.

- *Apartment or House.* Put your razor in the shower. Make sure you have an ample supply of toilet paper, shampoo, soap, and so on, so you aren't always running to get just one thing at the store. Again, keep track of when you are running low on things so you can get them on your next scheduled errand day. This will save you time, money, and probably a little bit of your sanity!

NOTE: If you find that you are resistant to doing any of the above, be aware that you are setting up roadblocks for your own success. Continually "forgetting" your gym clothes so you can't exercise is a form of self-sabotage. Be your own best friend, and set yourself up for success!

Prioritize Your Workload

Professionals with strong brands are those who are perceived as getting the job done. Flakiness and being undependable are brand killers no matter who you are. This is where prioritizing your workload comes in. This is important, because if you don't, you won't get the right things done and you will be perceived as flaky or undependable. This is most definitely not what you want.

So, if you can do this on your own, great. But even if you think you can do it on your own, I would still ask for help. Often we spend time on the wrong things, which is the opposite of how we want to spend our time. Start with your professors. Visit them in their offices, and ask them two questions:

1. If you were me, what would you do to make sure you succeeded in this class?

2. On this next assignment, what does an A look like?

As a professor, I can fill you in on the following secrets: (1) Professors *love* when students come in and ask questions like this, because we think that they care and that makes us really happy. (2) If you do this, professors really will help you prioritize your efforts for the course. We also might tell you what to *not* worry about, which is equally important.

You may have to visit your professor about question 2 each time there is an assignment, or you might get enough information during this first session to help you throughout the term.

Also, review the point scale on each syllabus. Things are weighted differently, so pay attention to this.

A Story

My brother and his engineering classmates were hard at work on a robot the week of finals, but they were all stressed, as they weren't finding time to study for the final exam. One of the students decided to look at the syllabus and found out the robot was worth 10 percent of their grade while the final was worth 40 percent. Needless to say, the majority of the rest of their efforts went toward studying, not tinkering. Everyone got the grade they wanted. Their robot didn't get an A, but that was less important than their overall course grade.

Also make sure you talk to your boss(es). Ask for a quick meeting, and ask them these questions:

1. What are the most important goals for our unit?

2. In your opinion, what tasks or areas that I am responsible for help the most toward achieving those goals?

3. On these particular tasks, what does success look like?

4. About how long do you think these things should take me? (This avoids over- and under-effort.)

Then use all of this wonderful, useful, relevant information to craft your priority list. This way, you only spend time on what really matters to the people that can help you achieve your goals. Many of us spend a great deal of time on things that don't have much value. Remember the economic term *ROI*—return on investment. Is your to-do list full of things with a high ROI? If not, make a new list.

Ask for Help If You Need It

If you don't know how to do something, find help. First, try to figure it out yourself, perhaps via a Google search or via asking someone in your network for some assistance. I ask Google things all the time. Sometimes I have great results, and sometimes I don't. See if you can find a YouTube video, or look on many of the how-to websites out there. Even if your Internet search doesn't get you a perfect picture of what you need to do, at least it might clarify some things and give you a better indication of what you do and don't know about this project or problem.

> NOTE: Now is a great time to talk about source credibility. Just because it is on the Web doesn't mean that it is true. Be conscious of where you are getting your information, and do the best you can to assess whether the source is credible. If you need some training in this area, visit your campus library. Librarians are a little lonely these days thanks to all of our online research, and it's also their job to help you. I guarantee that you will get all the help you need.

If this doesn't get you where you need to be, ask for help. The problem with this is that many of us are stubborn. And even if you aren't stubborn, most of us get embarrassed when we don't know how to do something. Just about all of us get nervous about calling attention to our deficiencies, and some of us are just plain clueless about our skillset. Unless you fall into this last category, I want you to read this next sentence very carefully. *Asking for help can assist you in building your brand.* Yep, that's right. Asking for help is a good thing, not a bad one. Here is why:

- People would much rather you ask for help to do things right the first time than have to redo your bad work or work with you to redo it.

- Asking for help shows you care about doing things correctly.

- Most people like to teach. It makes them feel smart and important.

- Humility is endearing.

- Know-it-alls are not.

So, ask for help. Ask for clarification. Ask for an example. Get what you need to be successful. Make sure you know all about length, depth, resources, and so forth before you begin. Here are some ways to ask for help:

- "I have a couple of questions about this project. When can I have a few minutes with you to talk about this?"

- "Excuse me. I know that this project is important, so I want to make sure I do it correctly. Can we talk about the steps you'd like me to use?"

- "Do you have an example that I could look at so I can get an idea of what direction to start with?"

Time Frames and Timers

When you start working on something, unless it really is just for fun and you have all of the time in the world, give yourself some time parameters. Ranges are good. Decide on the minimum and maximum time you'll spend on this particular thing, and then do it.

Use a timer so you don't have to clock watch. Clock watching is a huge time- and life-sucking activity. Setting up ranges gives you flexibility, and you can stop at the minimum if you feel you should, and you can keep going until the maximum if you are on a roll.

Within these time frames you can take little breaks if you find that is helpful for your productivity. Just be sure to use a timer for your breaks as well so you get back on track when you want to.

Chunk It

When you've got a big project, chunk it into smaller pieces. And make the chunks easy to accomplish. This will help you avoid procrastination and actually make progress. You can chunk work, school, or personal goals. For example, if you want to get in shape, don't start out with a marathon. Start out with running a few feet, and then walking a bit, and then running a little more, and then walking a bunch. The next day, add a little bit more running. You get the idea. Small, easy-to-implement steps are ironically the fastest path to success and one of the best ways to kill the procrastination bug.

Acceptable vs. Perfect

Another way to kill the procrastination bug is to know the difference between *acceptable* and *perfect*. Perfection is often an excuse for procrastination. You might delay starting something because you are worried about how to do it perfectly. This is ironic, you might notice, because procrastination is probably the best way to guarantee imperfection. But we are human, and that's what humans do.

The first thing you want to do is to figure out if what you want or have to do needs to be perfect or simply acceptable. But note that this is not an either-or proposition. Think of these things on a continuum—acceptable on one end and perfection on the other. How close to either side should this task or project be? Are you performing heart surgery? You might want it to be as close to perfect as you can be. Are you making a sandwich? Acceptable is probably fine. Making a sandwich for your future mother-in-law? Move a little closer to perfection. You get the idea. Once you decide, you can go from there, giving the appropriate time and effort to the task. We often skew toward perfection when we only need to skew toward acceptable, and this doesn't get us toward our goals.

Be a PS, Not a PI

The world is full of PIs (problem identifiers), so if you are a PS (problem solver), you can stand out and shine.

A Story

Several years ago, my family threw my parents a retirement party. It was at their house, and many, many people had been invited, and we were catering it ourselves. So as my husband, children, and I were in the kitchen chopping, mixing, and baking, one of our other family members was in the other room sitting on the couch watching TV. This couch happened to be next to a table where the guest book was for the party. This family member noticed that there was not a pen near the guest book, so he called into the other room, "Hey, the guest book needs a pen." We all did what you would have probably done—ignored him. A little while later, we heard from the other room again, "Hey, the guest book needs a pen." Again, we ignored him. Sometime later, with his voice a little more agitated, the family member called out, "Hey, the guest book needs a pen!" Clearly annoyed, my then-nine-year-old daughter stormed over to the pen drawer, grabbed a pen, walked into the other room, slammed down the pen, glared at the family member, and went back to her food-preparation duties.

Amused by the whole thing, I realized instantly that this story illustrates the PS/PI point beautifully. My daughter is a problem solver. She got the job done. My family member was being a problem identifier, pointing out what needed to be done but not doing it. Don't be like that. If you see something that needs to be done, do it. Put up extra chairs and move tables around the room to set up for the meeting if things aren't right when you get there.

The world is full of problem identifiers. They are the proverbial dime a dozen, and they are everywhere. You see them in Congress, you see them writing letters to the editor and calling in on all of those radio talk shows. I am certain that you also have plenty of them in your life.

And, in my opinion, they are worthless . . . unless they are also problem solvers.

Using the 75/25 Rule to Become a PS

There are two key verbs to being a problem solver: *anticipate* and *initiate*. By spending 75 percent of your time thinking and 25 percent doing, you'll start to anticipate things more. You'll start to see what has to happen in order for things to get done, and you'll start to see problems that need to be solved before most people do. Your anticipation abilities are like a muscle—they'll get stronger the more you use them.

Once you anticipate that something needs to be done, do it! This is where *initiate* comes in. Employers tell me almost daily how important it is to have employees who are *able* and *willing* to take initiative. Being able to act is the first step, and you won't be able to have initiative unless you employ the 75/25 rule. Being a problem solver takes thinking, and a lot of it. You must think about things like the following:

- What steps need to happen in order for this to get done?

- When should these steps take place?

- What problems might come up, and how do I solve them?

- Who else needs to be involved?

- If this has been done in the past, what resources still exist for me to use?

- What questions do I need to ask in order to move forward?

- Are there permissions or confirmations I need to secure?

Once you do your thinking, and know what needs to be done, you need to be willing to do it. Being willing is completely different than being able, and something most people struggle with. The reasons are plentiful. Sometimes you might lack confidence, or ability, or perhaps you are being just plain lazy, or skewing in that direction. Regardless, being willing to take initiative is essential, for what I hope are obvious reasons.

Let's start with the lack-of-confidence issue. Often this lack of confidence comes from fear—the fear of doing it wrong, fear of getting in trouble, fear of stepping on someone's toes, fear of . . . (you get the point). To get rid of fear, you need to start with accessing its validity. Is this a fear you should have? If so, how can you mitigate it? Usually communication will do this. Ask permission, keep people in the loop, circle back and let people know what you are doing. If yours is an unrealistic fear, dismiss it and move on.

Other times lack of confidence comes from lack of ability. You don't know how to do something, or you are not good at something. If this is the case, ask for help, or if you assess that you can't screw things up completely if you fail, just do it! People rarely get in trouble for trying to solve a problem, even if they don't get it exactly right. Most employers would rather have ten employees who tried and failed than one hundred who pointed out the problem and did nothing to fix it.

If you are just being lazy . . . well, I think you know how to fix this one. Suck it up and do it.

There are going to be times, of course, when you can't be a problem solver, but you can certainly be more than just a problem identifier. You can work *toward* solving the problem. If you really want to be successful, never come to someone with a problem that you have identified unless you have at least an idea for a solution. Your solution might not be *the* solution, but it will certainly get things moving forward on the right track. Your stock will always rise in this situation, whereas if you just come to people with problems that you have found, you'll become someone that people avoid.

A Story

My youngest daughter, like most children, gets distracted easily and hates doing chores. When I gave her a task, she would do the minimum and then want to get back to playing. So, with a chore like taking out the garbage, I had to teach her about anticipating and initiating, and she had to learn to finish the job with regard to her chores. It wasn't just about taking the garbage in the kitchen (and the recycling) outside and putting it in the big containers, it was about putting new liners in them and putting them back where they came from. It was also about emptying the small garbage cans in each bathroom, the one in the office, and the one in the laundry room. She (fairly quickly) got the idea, and I was extremely proud when I told her to take the dog outside to "take care of business" before we left him inside for the day (it gets very hot in Central California in the summers). She did as I asked, but she also filled up his water bowls and locked the back doors. She anticipated the related chores that had to be done before we could leave, used initiative to do them, and made life easier for everyone.

Most of the time your boss isn't going to give you step-by-step directions, and your professors often won't as well. An instructor might give you the desired outcome, or step one, but it'll be up to you to figure out the rest. If you want to succeed and move up quickly, you need to use the 75/25 rule, anticipate what else needs to be done, and use initiative to do it.

Whether dealing with your professor, boss, boyfriend or girlfriend, or family member, make sure you are a problem solver, not a problem identifier. Better yet, just fix the problem, and don't bother talking about it at all. You'll be recognized—don't worry—especially if you make this a habit. You'll get the reputation for being the one who just gets it done, and this type of reputation is invaluable.

Initiative in the Classroom

It's actually pretty easy to impress your professors by showing initiative in the classroom. Many times your professors will not give you all the instructions needed. Sometimes this is an oversight, and sometimes we do it on purpose, to see which students will shine.

A Story

In my beginning public relations course the students spend twenty-five hours during the semester doing a service-learning assignment with a local nonprofit organization. The students choose from a list of about thirty-five organizations, contact the organization, offer to volunteer in a PR capacity, fill out some paperwork by a deadline, and then complete their required hours and turn in a paper. It's a pretty straightforward assignment, but on the list of choices I often omit either the phone number or the e-mail address of the contact, and sometimes I include contact information that is incorrect. This is an unofficial test of sorts, as this exercise separates the students with initiative from those who don't have it.

Those with initiative:

- Find the information they need without asking my help.
- Notice the errors, find out the correct information, and then let me know for future reference.

Those without initiative:

- Get frustrated when they don't get an e-mail back, and when I ask if they also called their contact, they say that they were not given a phone number.
- Notice the errors and ask me to fix them.

There isn't any grade penalty or reward for this part of the assignment, but I do notice, and the results do influence my perception of the student's credibility as a future professional.

This is a simple example, but I have found that these are the small ways you can separate yourself from everyone else. Have initiative. If an Internet link is broken, find the correct one. If information is needed to move forward on a project, find it. Become an indispensible resource by taking initiative.

Cheat Sheet

- Spend 75 percent of your time thinking and 25 percent of your time doing.
- Slow down.
- Define your Priorities Right Now.
- Use the compounding effect.
- Carve out time to think.
- Carve out time to do life/time reviews.
- Think before you start anything.
- Write it down.
- Enjoy the creativity bonus.
- Choose accuracy over speed.
- Kill the procrastination bug.
  - Get control of e-mail.
  - Establish limits for social media.
  - Set up your physical spaces.
  - Prioritize your workload.
  - Ask for help if you need it.
  - Use time frames and timers.
  - Chunk it.
  - Usually choose acceptable over perfect.
- Be a problem solver, not a problem identifier.

MASTER EVERY CONVERSATION
Professor Hays

W e all have many conversations every day. Some are planned, and many are not. Conversations can be helpful, stressful, boring, or inspiring, and most of the time we think this happens by chance. Starting today, don't leave these outcomes to chance. Be purposeful and strategic when you talk to others, and you'll see your goals come to fruition very quickly. This chapter includes detailed instructions for mastering every conversation, tying in our previous ideas of building your brand, immersing yourself, and employing the rule of 75 percent thinking to 25 percent doing.

Clarify Your Goal

If you don't know what your goal is in a conversation, you are not likely to achieve it. To set yourself up for success and master *every* conversation, first figure out what you want to accomplish before you engage. Possible conversation goals could include the following:

- a lead for an internship
- advice on what classes to take
- a date
- the name of the best local pizza place

- a tip for a good website to use to host or build your blog

- some names to build your network

- thoughts on which of two professors is best

- to sound intelligent so this person will want to continue networking with you

- to enjoy a few minutes of conversation with someone interesting before class begins

- to test out public perception of a thought you just had regarding an issue

You get the idea. The goal doesn't always have to be life changing or earth saving; it just needs to be known, and known to you. While obviously some of these goals have more value than others toward your ultimate life success, all of them are perfectly acceptable goals for conversations. The important thing is that you *have* a goal and that you are conscious of it. If you don't, you significantly decrease the chances of getting what you want.

Once you have your goal, you can move on, but not until then.

Know Your Audience

The notion of knowing your audience is a staple in the public relations world, and it should also be a staple in all of your conversations. Knowledge of your audience—whether that audience is a professor, a fellow student, or a prospective employer—can lead to getting what you want out of every conversation.

How do you master every conversation? By knowing your audience and knowing them as intimately as possible (without crossing privacy boundaries, of course). Prior to talking to anyone, think about what you know about them. What's their conversational style? Do they want all the details or just the headlines? Do they like to chat first or just get to the point? What are they interested in? What are their priorities? What makes them angry? What are their habits and interests that relate to this topic? You want to know what your audience thinks about things, why they think those things about things, and what their usual habits are. You also want to know what they care about, what they don't care about, and what things bug them, what motivates them, what doesn't motivate them, and anything else you can think of.

The more you know about your audience—whether it is an audience of one or thousands—the better you can connect, the better your relationships will be, and the more you can use every conversation to move you closer to your goals.

So how do you get this knowledge? Past experience is wonderful, of course. Absent that, you can have conversations with others about your audience, look at their social media posts, their past performances or job histories, and so forth. You can do an Internet search and also observe them, if that is feasible (without, of course, appearing like a stalker).

Offer Something of Value

Once you've done your thinking (or your research, if you don't know the person you are going to talk to very well), you can tie this knowledge in to what you want from this conversation by figuring out how you can offer this person something of value. Offering someone something of value helps increase your chances of getting what you want.

As you are aware, people like to connect with people they like, and one of the best ways to get someone to like you is to be a provider of information of value and not be just a taker. One-sided relationships—whether friendships, romantic relationships, or professional ones—rarely last. No one wants to feel like they are doing all the giving and the other person is doing all of the taking. As you have probably personally experienced, this gets old, and it gets old fast.

Think about what you know that could be of value to the person you are talking to. What do you know about that they don't? You are probably interested in many things and might even know more about some of them than most people do. Be aware of this, and use this to your advantage. If you position yourself as a source of value, you will be valued.

You may know a lot about cooking or comic books or sci-fi movies or video games or website creation or college football or nineteenth-century paintings of horses or high-end sports cars. You many know nothing about any of those things, but you know a lot about something else. Everyone has pockets of knowledge, because we tend to acquire knowledge about things that we are really interested in, and everyone is interested in something. Whatever you are passionate about you tend to become an expert in. Often others will be interested as well. You might be funny or a wonderful artist or a whiz with knitting needles. You might have a green thumb or a way with animals or a knack for putting together exactly the right outfit.

Share some of this information, and this can be your something-of-value.

Sometimes during the course of a conversation you might not have the opportunity to offer something of value. This is okay. Listen attentively (which actually is offering something of *tremendous* value), and then try to circle back later with a link to something that could offer value after the fact. For example, you might see an article or photo that relates to your prior conversation and send it via e-mail or even Twitter. Twitter is better, frankly, as you can then indirectly share with others and publicly show how you put effort into helping out people in your network—increasing your value. You can also tag people in social media posts that relate to things that you have discussed as well, further sharing value and also letting them know that you are thinking of them, making them feel important. You can add a note that says something like "Thought you might find this interesting" or "Per our conversation, here's another idea (or perspective or thought)." This, frankly, is the easiest way to add value, but it takes strategic effort, therefore being one more thing on your list of things that most people don't do (and an opportunity for you to stand out).

A Story

During a visit to the zoo last summer I was interviewed via phone by a newspaper reporter for comment about a local brand involved in a marketing lawsuit. My daughter and I had come to the zoo in part because there was media coverage that morning about sea lions being placed in a new exhibit that was about to open. I mentioned this to the reporter, and he told me he was going to bring his son to the zoo later that week to see the sea lions in their new home. After I hung up, I discovered that the sea lions had been moved back out of the exhibit so it could be finished. When we got home, I sent a quick e-mail to the reporter, alerting him that he should double-check the sea lions' location prior to going to the zoo, helping him and his son avoid disappointment. Value added. Relationship strengthened.

Have a Stash of Conversation Fuel

One of the best ways to always make sure you have something of value to share (a.k.a. *conversation fuel*) is to become a "news junkie." People who keep up with what's happening in the world—locally, nationally, and internationally—are simply more interesting than people who don't. The wonderful thing about living in today's world is that you don't even have to watch the news or read a newspaper to be a news junkie. You can follow news outlets on Twitter, like them on Facebook, use their or other mobile apps, or visit their or other websites.

Interesting things are happening in the world all the time, and it's up to you to be aware of them and use these tidbits as conversation fuel. A comment about the weather will always get you started, but if that's all the fuel you have, you will see the conversation die quickly. You've got to stoke conversations like you stoke fires—with lots of fuel!

You might be thinking, *There are a lot of news stories out there, but how do I know which ones would be good conversation fuel?* Here are some guidelines about what to look for:

1. Does the story matter? If a story has significant consequence to a lot of people or matters to the person you are talking to or a group they belong to, it's great fuel.

2. Does anybody care? If a story is interesting to you, it probably is interesting to others. Great fuel.

3. Is the story about something new or different? If something is new, it could be great fuel. If something is odd, unique, or different, it's probably better fuel.

4. Is the story about something that happened nearby? Local stories are usually of more interest to people. A huge corporate layoff three states away is not as interesting as a smaller one closer to home.

5. Did it happen recently, or is it happening now? People care about what has happened in the very recent past or is happening right now or will happen in the not-too-distant future. That's why they call them *current* events.

6. Is the story hot? The media, like the rest of us, gets obsessed with things. You have probably encountered a time when you thought to yourself, "I wish the media would stop talking about [topic]," or "If I read, see, or listen to one more story about [topic] I will scream!" Ironically, you can use this to your advantage. If a story has been covered for a while, more people will be aware of it, and more people will be talking about it. Know what these hot topics are, and you'll have a steady stream of good fuel.

7. Is someone famous involved? The celebrity factor counts for a lot in the discussion of conversation fuel. As evidenced by the growing popularity of websites, blogs, and TV programs that report celebrity gossip, we as a society love this stuff. Knowledge of current stories regarding celebrities, local or otherwise, can be great fuel, even if you use it in an ironic way (i.e., "I can't believe how much news coverage [name of celebrity] is getting for [dumb thing he or she did]").

Elevator Pitches

A useful tool for conversation mastery is the elevator pitch.

The idea of an elevator pitch comes from the world of entrepreneurship. It comes from the idea of actually being in an elevator and only having a short amount of time to pitch your idea to someone. The thought is, of course, that your pitch is so brilliant that the person you are talking to forgets all about their original destination and continues with you in the elevator to talk with you about your business, product, or service, and, at the end of the ride, you've secured a sale or a new vendor or a new contact that will lead to a sale.

When you are in an elevator, there is no time for wasted words—hence the crux of the concept of elevator pitches. They need to be to the point, or you'll lose the opportunity.

I like to think of an elevator pitch as a structured, rehearsed way of talking about whatever you want to talk about, keeping in mind your conversation goal. And I believe that elevator pitches are an idea we should use more frequently. As you already know, every encounter we have should be an opportunity to advance our goals.

Think about it. We get asked all the time, "How are you?" or "What's new?" And usually we answer, "Fine" or "Busy" or "Same old, same old" or some other equally lame version of one of these. Sometimes we even answer in a way that might scare people or encourage them to stop talking to us, like "Crazy busy!" or "You don't even want to know!" or "Oh, my goodness, it would take all day to tell you about my drama." Do these answers help us accomplish any of our goals? I don't think so either. This means there are dozens of opportunities every day that we are not maximizing. In fact, there are dozens of opportunities every day that might actually be harming our ability to achieve our goals.

To start maximizing these opportunities, create polished and succinct responses to all of your typical conversation scenarios. Think about the questions you typically get asked, and write down some better answers. By *better answers*, I mean ones that will help you reach your goals. Think about what you want, as well as your brand, and use these as the raw materials for your "elevator pitches."

For example, you need to have a response to some or all of these questions:

- "How is school?"

- "What do you want to do after graduation?"

- "How are you?"

- "How was your day?"

- "What's new?"

The Three Cs

Here are the three secrets of elevator pitch success—otherwise known as the three Cs. Your elevator pitch(es) must be (1) clear, (2) concise, and (3) consistent.

CHAPTER FIVE

Clear

In a world of short attention spans and unlimited competition for our time and attention, you know as well as I do that when people are confused they'll do one of two things: (1) tune out or (2) move on. The best way to *not* achieve your conversation goals is to be confusing. If people can't understand you, they'll move on to the next, whether that is the next person they have an opportunity to talk to or the next thing that pops into their head. And they'll stop listening, which is a horrible and embarrassing end to any conversation.

Ways to be more clear include making sure that your language matches that of the person you are talking to. Don't use slang, jargon, or words they don't understand. Statistics, anecdotes, and analogies are also great ways to increase clarity. Statistics are great because they help explain magnitude, impact, or depth of a topic or issue. Be careful, though. If you rattle off too many statistics at once, you will lose people and again they will tune out. Anecdotes are helpful as well because everyone loves stories. And when a story is brief and relevant, it can be a wonderful way to explain an idea. Just keep your stories on the short side. And try to avoid having to say, "and to make a long story longer . . ." Analogies are also excellent tools, for if you can explain a complex idea by comparing it to something that the person you are talking to understands, he or she will have many more aha moments.

Concise

Use as few words as possible to convey your message. Why? We all have really short attention spans.

Consistent

Once you decide on what you want to say, say it frequently. Be consistent with your elevator pitches and you'll notice that your brand gets stronger and your goals get closer to completion.

Elevator-Pitch Content

Let's take each of the questions you are usually asked and come up with some ideas for your elevator pitches, keeping in mind your Priorities Right Now list as well as the brand you are trying to build.

Regarding your list of Priorities Right Now, what is the most important thing you are trying to accomplish? Could others help you get there? What information are you missing? What are you having trouble finding? Where are you encountering a dead-end? All of this thinking will help you craft the best response.

Regarding your brand, how can you use your elevator pitches to build yours? Remember the words you chose in chapter 2 that you want others to use to describe you. Your responses to these key questions can help people connect those words to you. This is where the consistency piece mentioned before really becomes important. When your elevator pitches are consistent with your brand, and are used frequently, you add strength to your brand.

Question 1: How Is School?

Again, *never again* do I want you to answer this question with "Fine" or "Horrible" or, worse, "So busy!" These are not ways to advance your goals. They are worthless comments and a waste of everyone's time. They can also harm your brand. Remember, these are not the words you chose for your brand, but when you repeatedly use them they are the words that people associate with you. If your mantra is "So busy!" whenever you are asked how you are, people are going to associate this with you more so than anything else. We are all busy. This isn't news, nor is it helpful. You're busy. We'll all assume that's the case. Tell us something we *don't* necessarily know.

So, how should you answer this question? Answer with a response that advances your goals. Examples:

- "Fantastic. This semester [quarter] my favorite class is [name], and we are working on [assignment]. I am really moving toward becoming a [dream job title]."

- "Really challenging. I'm into my core major classes, including [name], and we are working on [assignment] and [assignment]. It will be worth it, though, when I am a [dream job title]."

- "Wonderful. I'm really working hard, especially in [name of class], and I'm also looking for an internship in [industry]."

- "Great. Things are really making sense, especially in [name of class]. I'm also trying to build my network, including people who know more about [topic]."

- "Super. In fact, I'm about to start work on my senior project, [name of project], and am looking for [what you are looking for]."

A NOTE ABOUT MY EXAMPLES: Obviously, you'll want to customize these responses to make them sound like you. I happen to love the two words *awesome* and *wonderful*. (According to my family, I tend to even overuse those words, but they are authentic to me, and I feel comfortable using them.) You probably have words that are authentic to you, so incorporate those into your elevator pitches. These examples are purely provided to get you thinking about how you can use these ideas to help *you*, not to make you carbon copies of us.

How do these answers move you closer to your goals? They build your brand, they let people know who you are and what you are working toward, and they give people an opportunity to offer help. As we continue to tell you, people *love* students, and you need to take advantage of this while you still have the opportunity. With some good, brief, specific information like the above, if the person you are talking to knows someone or something that can move you forward, they will share it. It's almost like the universe makes them do it. When you answer "Fine," the person you are talking to is under no obligation to help you. So they won't, and you won't be moving forward. And forward, of course, is the direction we want to continually go.

Your turn: *What are you going to say the next time someone asks you, "How's school?"*

NOTE: This answer may change frequently depending on how quickly you reach your goals or how many goals you are working on at the same time. This is fine, and wonderful, frankly. Just be conscious about your responses at all times, and make sure they are working for you.

Question 2: What Do You Want to Do After Graduation?

This is a tough one, especially if you aren't entirely sure, but it's a question you will get, and get frequently, guaranteed.

Ideas for good answers:

- "Gosh, I'm still not sure, but I know I want to move to [location]. I am trying to find connections to people who live there so I can start to build my network."

- "Gosh, I'm still not sure, but I know it will be in the areas of [industry] or [industry], and I'm really looking for people to talk to who are already in those professions."

- "I want to be [name of dream career], and to get there I'm working hard to talk to as many people as possible who are already working in that field."

- "I am going to be [name of dream career]. I'm well on my way, but what I still need to do is [what you still need to do]."

- "Either [dream career] or [dream career]. Still exploring by [method of exploration]."

By now you are getting the idea, and these answers will lend themselves beautifully to your getting help moving forward. Worst case, you'll get a suggestion that you ultimately reject, but more likely you'll get an idea you can use, or you'll get a suggestion that leads to an idea that you can use.

Your turn: *What will you say the next time someone asks you, "What do you want to do after graduation?"*

NOTE: The closer you get to graduation, the more frequently you will get this question. Again, use this to your advantage. And, as always, humor can work in a pinch. Feel free to throw out a "I have no clue; do you want to support me?" every once in a while. You never know, right?

Question 3: How Are You?

Answers to this question are often the *worst* offenders for accomplishing nothing and the worst offenders for harming your brand. Horrible answers to this question are things like "Swamped," "Crazy busy," "Stressed," "Tired," or something similar. You might be all of those things, but the only one who really needs to ever hear those answers, and even then not all the time, are your best friend and your mom, and sometimes Grandma (if there might be chocolate-chip cookies involved to make you feel better). Everyone else needs to get your elevator pitch. Thoughts for better answers:

- "Oh, wow, there is so much good stuff going on! It's like drinking from a fire hose, but I am not complaining. The most fun thing I'm doing is [fun thing], and I am really trying to [goal that you have]."

- "Pretty darn good. I am [cool thing you are doing] and am working toward [goal that you have]."

- "Fantastic. Only thing that would make it better would be if I [need that you have]."

Question 4: How Was Your Day?

You might think we are harsh, but to recap one more time, there are *very few* people who really need or want the actual honest answer to this question, whatever that may be. Everyone else needs to get your elevator pitch. If you are sad or angry or frustrated or tired or whatever else, save it for your close circle of people and let them help you through it. Or let them be simply a place to vent. The world is not your place to vent, which obviously makes social media not the place to vent as well. (More on this in chapter 9.)

Your turn: Think quickly here, because this opportunity will probably come up later today. *What will you say the next time someone asks you, "How are you?" or "How was your day?"*

Think About What Other Answers You Need

You probably have other questions you get asked frequently. Think about them, and craft responses for each. Use them each and every time, and watch what happens. I promise that you'll see things in your life move forward very quickly if you never say "Fine" or "Busy" again!

Conversation Trees

If possible, include a *conversation tree* in your elevator pitches. This is when you use the magic words *and* or *or* to give people choices regarding advancing the conversation. When you provide a response that includes an *and* or an *or*, you are essentially providing your conversation partner with two or three metaphorical branches to choose from. This increases the likelihood of their moving in one of the directions you would like the conversation to go. Absent an *and*, the conversation might go elsewhere if the person you are speaking to has nothing to add or is not interested in the one branch you offered.

For example, you can share that you are working on project X and project Y. This gives the person you are talking to two choices to grab onto as you continue the conversation. If he or she has nothing to add regarding project X, maybe he or she knows something that could help with project Y. Or you can let people know that you are looking for an internship in industry X, Y, or Z. Bam! Three potential branches.

NOTE: Do not offer more than three branches at a time. Our attention spans are only so long!

More about the Magic Word *And*

I mentioned the magic word *and* above, but I want to share with you another magical element about it. No matter what question you are asked, in any conversation, you are always able to answer with one of your elevator pitches—all by using *and*.

Whatever you are asked, go ahead and answer the question, but before you verbally volley the conversation back to the person you are talking to, add something with an *and*. Sometimes the magic words *but* or *or* can help you do the same thing. Practice—it can be a fun challenge.

Some examples:

- "Yes, this pizza is amazing, and I don't want to forget to tell you that [whatever it is you want to share]."

- "No, I don't like that class at all, but I do love [class] and can't wait to try out those skills in my career. In fact, I really need to start looking for an internship . . ."

- "Wow, I really don't know, but I need to get going so I'm not late for my class/internship/meeting with my professor. We are talking about [topic], and I really want to learn more."

Put It All Together

Yes, we've talked about elevator pitches, which are all about the conversation staying about you, but you need to make sure that you are also remembering our previous discussions about offering value to those you talk to. When you skillfully combine these two elements, you become a valued conversation partner and someone who is constantly working toward both accomplishing your goals *and* building your network.

Ways to do this include the following:

- "Thanks so much for that tip. I've got one for you. You might want to check out [website] or [blog]. I think you might like it."

- "Wow, that's a great idea. Thank you. Let me know if you ever need [something you can offer]. I owe you!"

- "Cool. I will follow up with that. And I'll also let [person] know that you are interested in [whatever it is]."

More About Content

Earlier I asked you to always have a goal for every conversation. Here's another way to look at that challenge. Ask yourself, "After we are done talking, I want the person I'm having a conversation with to . . . what?" What do you want them to do? Be impressed? Offer you a job? Give you a lead? Clap? Laugh? Follow you on Twitter? What action are you looking for? This thinking can also help you plan for successful conversations.

Once you know what you want your conversant to do, you can work backward from there. An important item to keep in mind is to give people the How. If you want someone to pick you up from work, make sure they have the right address and directions. If you want someone to do their part of a group assignment, make sure they have the tools to do so and send them reminders of their parts and deadlines in writing via e-mail. Set the people in your life up to successfully do what you need them to do. This helps them and helps you, and we all love win-wins!

Something else to consider is the "So what?" question. Make sure you frequently articulate why what you are doing, or working toward, is a good thing, either for that person as an individual or for that particular industry or for the community or society as a whole. Answer the "So what?" question. Why should anyone care about what you are saying? If you don't know, figure it out or change what you are saying.

Some Guiding Thoughts

An elevator pitch is not a monologue; it's an invitation for dialogue. It's not a dissertation; it's a conversation. Be cautious not to open a conversation with a very long string of comments. Let the other person talk too.

Pay Attention to Outcomes

Once you've been using your knowledge of your audiences and your elevator pitches for a while in order to master every conversation, take stock of your outcomes. Which responses worked best? Which didn't work at all? Which scenarios made you most comfortable? Which made you uncomfortable?

Notice the difference between the times you chose a specific goal ahead of time and when you didn't. Pay attention to how quickly the conversation turned away from you when you didn't use conversation trees. Using this knowledge, adjust. And try new things. Experimentation is probably going to serve you better with regard to the content in this chapter far better than any other.

You might want to think of conversations as paintings. Painters try out new colors, and color combinations, to see what works best. Sometimes they use one color more than another, and on a different day it's just the opposite. Be like a painter. Use bold, specific things one day and subtle things the next. See what you like, and see what approaches work best for *you*. You might be like a portrait painter, very into details and specifics. Or you might be more like an abstract artist, preferring to discuss generalities first before getting down to specific business. Use the authentic *you* in your conversations. This will enable you to have the most success.

Also, remember why you are doing this. You are doing this because you are, starting today, never again going to waste an opportunity to have a human interaction help you achieve your goals. Never again will you answer "Nothing" or "Too much" or anything similar when someone asks you what you've been up to.

Cheat Sheet

- Clarify your goal.

- Know your audience.

- Offer something of value.

- Have a stash of conversation fuel.
  - Fuel-hunting guidelines:
    - Does the story matter?
    - Does anybody care?
    - Is the story about something new or different?
    - Is the story about something that happened nearby?

- Did it happen recently, or is it happening now?
- Is the story hot?
- Is someone famous involved?

- Create elevator pitches for the following questions:
  - How is school?
  - What do you want to do after graduation?
  - How are you?
  - How was your day?
  - What's new?

- Use the three Cs.
  - Clear
  - Concise
  - Consistent

- Create conversation trees.

- Use the magic words *and*, *but*, or *or*.

- Keep your outcome in mind.
  - What do you want to happen after you talk?

- Keep the "So what?" in mind.

- Monitor conversation outcomes, adjust, and be authentic.

INNOVATE TO STAND OUT
Tori

The main question to ask yourself in this chapter is, *How do I make myself stand out?* Now is when you need to show your stuff. Show that self-starter attitude, and find ways to showcase your talents.

A perfect way to show individual talent is to use initiative and create a space to learn. Find a way to practice and perfect your talents in a real-world but reasonably controlled environment. The point is for you to get creative and show the innovative nature that employers crave (and expect) from our generation.

Here are some ideas to get you started. Read them all, even if the heading doesn't appeal to you right away. You never know when a kernel of awesomeness is going to hit you in just the right way to make an impact or spark an idea that will propel your success.

Start a Business

Starting a business is a great way to help you stand out. Not many college-aged people are actual entrepreneurs, and this will enable you to show future employers that you have initiative, a self-starter mentality, and the ability to do research and overcome obstacles—all highly sought-after skills in any industry.

For me, innovating meant starting my own business. I went to college in an area that didn't have a wide variety of options for internships, and I wanted to make sure I gained as much experience as I could to differentiate myself from other soon-to-be new grads. I decided after a few internships that starting my own business would be a great way to expand my expertise and also make some cash. I also found my first client by tapping into the student business incubator—a nonprofit center on campus that helps students start their own businesses. It was a win-win for both of us because I provided public relations services at a discount to students and they trusted me because we were on the same level. Through my business I was able to gain a lot of experience very quickly. I also used my editing skills to offer college-paper and graduate-thesis editing, which students loved and became a great way to for me to hone critical skills.

Do I think that all students need to start their own businesses? No. Should you? Sure! It's great for you to make money and gain experience and new skills, and it helps the economy. It's the trifecta of good stuff. I believe that anyone can start their own business, and it definitely makes it *much* more fun to go to work; there's no boss to tell you what to do. *You* are the boss! And you may have heard this before, but if you can find what you love to do and do it for a living, you'll never suffer that feeling of "having to go to work." Trust me—that freedom is one of the best feelings in the world. I strive every day to make sure I feel that way, and if I don't, then I start to actively think about how to change my position.

Starting a business really isn't as scary as it sounds. Most people think it is a huge undertaking, but please don't let that scare you from this section of the book. *Your* business can be built around anything you like to do. If you are an engineering major, use your training in computer-aided drafting programs to make professional sketches and detailed designs for landscape or home improvement. If you are an event-planning major, offer to help friends and family with small events, parties, or weddings. Marketing major? Offer your consulting services for a fee. Studying math? Create a tutoring service.

First, make sure you check out the requirements in your area (business license, taxes, etc.) before you start taking payment for anything. Check your state, city, and county requirements; the Internet is a great resource for this, and a quick phone call can generally get you all the information that you need. Many college campuses and communities have business incubators—as I mentioned earlier—that are wonderful resources. SCORE is a great source of free information (www.score.org).

Next, put together your business plan. This probably sounds intimidating, but it doesn't need to be a huge, drawn-out document. In fact, it should be a document that is quick and to the point. Writing a business plan is important because it helps you organize your thoughts and really nail down why you are starting this business. It also makes others take you more seriously—especially if you do need any financial help, or seed money, to get started. You'll definitely need a business plan to get money from anyone besides your parents.

The main things to keep in mind when deciding to put together a business plan are (1) what your customers or clients need and how you fulfill that need and (2) why your solution is better than anyone else's. Then make sure your business plan includes the following sections:

1. *Brief business description.* Seriously, this should be one paragraph; keep it simple!

2. *Management team.* It is totally fine if this is only you, but why are you the best? Remember your brand from chapter 2 here.

3. *Business objective.* What is the problem, and how does your business solve it?

4. *Your market.* How big is it? How much do they spend? Who are they?

5. *Overview of your product.* Make this simple and clear. Use diagrams and pictures, if possible.

6. *Value proposition.* Why is your product or business unique?

7. *Business model.* How are you going to make money? How will you reach your market (advertising, etc.)? What is your projected revenue? Be realistic.

8. *Competitor analysis.* Who are your competitors? Why are you better?

Also, within your business plan you should figure out your logo, mission, and goals. Keep the business plan as a guideline, and realize that it is just that—a *guideline*. It will take a lot of research and several revisions to get it right. Feel free to change as you continue to grow and expand your business, product, and services.

A Story

I ran into the need for a business plan when starting the student-run public relations firm at my college with a few of my peers. We approached a professional organization that partnered with one of our student organizations and asked them for seed money to get our on-campus office up and running with business cards for all employees, office supplies, and so forth. We were able to raise the amount of money we needed because we came prepared, knew what we needed, and presented our case well. It's the same in any start-up business: People are willing to invest time or money to help you if the return on investment is worth it for them.

After composing your business plan, you need to research your market and what you should charge for goods and services. As I mentioned in chapter 3, my friend started a fashion business and then started calling other possible real-world competitors to ask them their price points. If you do this, make sure you let them know that you are a student researching the market and are excited to get into their field. What's also important here is to remember that you are a student, not a seasoned veteran, so price your goods and services accordingly. You shouldn't charge what someone with a degree and experience is charging. Start prices low, grow your client base, and then slowly raise your rates as you become more and more busy. When your time is in demand or your goods are running low you can charge more because people will still come to you. It's all about supply and demand here. Think about Disneyland: They raise their rates often, charging quite a bit more than other theme parks for their tickets, but their park still fills up and they make a lot of money because people want to go—what they offer is in demand.

Here are a few things to consider when starting a service business (as opposed to a product business).

Project Fees

Consider charging by project instead of by the hour. I know that several highly respected professions still charge by the hour, but the idea seems so old-fashioned to me, especially in the era of multitasking and being able to work 24-7 from anywhere. If you charge by the hour, and then spend five minutes here and there throughout the day working on a project, it's easy to lose track of that time or know how to adequately charge for it. Project fees work best because then you know what you'll be earning for a project, the customer knows what they will be paying, and you'll all be happier in the end. Not to brag too much, but I work really quickly. Frankly, I have found that I work faster than most people. So when I charge clients by the hour, I usually lose. I also, being a millennial, work on several things at a time, as you probably do. This also makes by-the-hour billing challenging. Figure out what a fair project fee is for the project you are being asked to do, charge that, and complete it in however much time it takes you to do it. This is much easier for you, and less time is wasted tracking time.

The Hassle Tax

When you have your own business, you have the freedom to charge what you want. This is where we explore a great concept that I learned from my coauthor: the idea of a *hassle tax*. You'll start to learn that certain clients require a lot more of your time. When clients want you to redo the same thing four times or take a long time to pay you, you might consider whether or not you want to charge them more for your grief and stress level. Charge what you think is appropriate as your hassle tax for these clients. (Clearly, this term won't show up on your invoice, but this idea will help you be more cheerful when working on these projects.) Also, if you are in a fee-for-service business, consider not making your fees public so that you can charge each client appropriately. If you love a client, believe in what they are doing, enjoy what you do for their project, or feel that the experience is worth a lot to your résumé or portfolio, you may choose to charge those clients less. It's all up to you—you're the boss!

Then keep your overhead low by working out of your house or apartment or asking your university if they have any incentives for student businesses. Order business cards online to hand out, and then use your network to get your name out there. Let everyone know your services are available and that you are looking for the chance to prove what you've got. You should also develop a simple website and perhaps some social media sites as well (more on these in chapter 9).

Paperwork

You should always have some type of paperwork, even if it's simple, to track the money that flows in and out of your business. This includes letters of agreement (simple contracts) to keep with your clients, invoices that you use so you and your client both have a record of what was paid and when, and simple record keeping with receipts, mileage used, and so on. This paperwork makes you look (and feel) much more organized and prepared. And when tax time comes you'll thank yourself for being so proactive; you won't have to dig back through bank statements and stacks of paperwork to find what you charged someone. Then you can look at all of your records and decide what could be tax deductible among the things that you had to pay out of your own pocket. Things that are generally tax deductible include office supplies, gas used for business purposes (the IRS gives you a set rate per mile), portions of your rent if you designate a specific office space used only for work, and much more.

Tip: Don't have any idea where to start with paperwork? Go online and search for sample letters of agreement, contracts, and the like in your field. You'll be amazed at what pops up to help you. Generally Microsoft Office Word online templates have plenty of samples of simpler documents for you to look through as well. Review several, research the best way to use them, and decide which documents work best for you.

If you start your own business, please go to the IRS website and learn more about tax deductions. It can save you a lot of money, and you can be sure to get the most out of your business. You can also seek the advice of a professional accountant or bookkeeper. This is definitely case of "better safe than sorry," so be sure you are familiar with exactly what you need to do prior to filing your taxes.

You're the Boss

Now is when your work ethic is *very* important. You don't have a boss telling you what to do. There aren't any professors grading your work.

You have to be committed enough to devote the time and energy to it. When you have a project due to a client, you need to make sure that is your priority—not going out to see that new movie or spending time with the cute guy or girl that caught your eye that day. Definitely still make time for fun, but realize that every client you have is your most important client. If you have one bad review, it can cut off an entire part of your network and burn a lot of bridges. Plus, it's embarrassing. Give yourself enough time to make sure that every piece of work you develop is your best piece of work. Even though you'll probably be paid anyway, and no one is there to grade anything, it is important that you prove your worth in your work and the projects you complete. These are your real-world projects that will stand out in your résumé and portfolio. It's what makes you stand out!

When you are meeting with clients, make sure that you stick to your gut. I'm sure you know that "icky" feeling that you get in your gut when you meet certain people. Trust it. Understand that you can't work with everyone, and some people may just not be worth it. Save yourself some heartache in the long run by trusting your gut and only working with clients whom you feel good about working with. I'll skip the horror stories here (maybe we'll put them in the next book). Just trust yourself to know when to say no. The best way to say no, without slandering anyone, is to simply say that you are too busy to take on more work at the moment, but you wish them well with their adventures.

NOTE FROM PROFESSOR HAYS: You might even want to set up a litmus test here. For example, I don't take on anyone as a client that I wouldn't want to introduce to my children. Unfortunately, how I came to have this rule was one of the horror stories Tori references above. Once I didn't trust my gut and came very close to taking on a client that turned out to be not the kind of person I would want my professional brand associated with. It was a really unsettling experience, and it led me to my litmus test, which has never let me down!

Travel

Another great way to innovate and learn a lot outside of the classroom is to travel. Meeting new people and seeing things from different perspectives is more valuable than I could ever articulate to you here. Once you've done it, you'll understand.

And don't worry if you aren't rolling in the dough; this can be where your in-depth involvement in student and professional associations can come to your rescue. Many student associations have large conferences, and you can apply via your major department or your university to help fund your trip. I received funding through my student association to attend a national conference, which was huge for my budding career.

Don't think that traveling means that you need to see the world in order to start that career; in fact, sometimes it's hard to get your career started if you are traveling around too much. If you have a great internship, have started your business, or really feel that nurturing your network is more important, balance your priorities and decide what is best for you. The point is to travel enough so that you feel like you have a better understanding of your career path from many different places (some parts of the country or world may have a totally different market for your chosen career).

Domestic Travel

Traveling domestically is a great way to see new places, discover what parts of your country you like better and why, learn where you want to live and work, meet new people to add to your network, and meet your soon-to-be competition in the job market.

Let's start with seeing new places. Who doesn't love to travel? Even if it's just for a weekend or a week, you'll get to see things you've never seen before and experience a whole different lifestyle. I don't care if it's just state to state or county to county—if you really pay attention, you will notice some huge (and some not-so-huge but important) differences in cultures. For example, someone I work with is from Colorado, and when she moved to the Bay Area in California she was shocked by the fact that no one holds doors open for anyone—at least not very often. Now holding doors open is not a big difference in culture, nor would it have much effect on your job performance, but if manners are extremely important to you, it could sway you to move somewhere else.

If you stick around a new area long enough, you'll definitely get a better understanding of what kinds of places you like to be and the types of people you like to be around. This will help you decide where you want to live and work. This could mean living with an aunt, grandparent, or friend for a summer internship in a "faraway place." During the summer you'll get a chance to experience the climate, culture, personalities, activities, entertainment, and overall excitement of a place you think you might want to live in. This is a great way to experience a new city or state, because once you graduate it's hard to experience different places without setting down roots. Employers tend to not want to hire college graduates for only three months; it costs a lot to train you! But if you're a student, you have this great excuse to go back to your comfort zone at college at the end of the summer and think hard about whether or not you want to make the move. I bet that employer would also love for you to come back after graduation (or the following summer); you've been trained, you understand the job, and they already know you rock at it.

When you travel you will meet new people. In fact, traveling is a great way to get out there and meet a lot of different kinds of people, while in school or even after graduation. Meeting people is great for many things, but most relevant to this book is networking. Read more on this in chapter 8.

A Warning

One of the not-so-fun things about getting out there and meeting your soon-to-be competitors is that you will meet people smarter than you, and this is no fun at all. In fact, it sucks. There will be those that have a much more impressive résumé, are way more experienced, and seem to have it all figured out. That doesn't mean you should go in with war paint on your face and start sabotaging anyone you meet.

When you do meet people like this, put your best foot forward. Seek those smarter people out. Understand that these are the people you need in your network. They will ground you. They will be the amazing references and connections that will help you get your foot in the door with companies you've only dreamed of. Don't be threatened. The smart people are those who keep even smarter people in their network. You should too. We'll cover this in greater detail later.

And, to help your self-esteem, do note that sometimes first impressions are deceiving. You will end up being way more awesome than many of these people, and that's not a bad thing either!

International Travel

Traveling internationally can also be a great experience. I know several people who think it was one of the best things they've ever done. Study abroad programs are a fantastic way to do this and can get you into a classroom with international students who are just as curious and ready to conquer the world as you are.

A Story

A friend of mine, Taylor, knew she wanted to be a teacher and spent a semester abroad in Austria. While there she fell in love with the culture, people, and places. When she got back from her overseas study program she started tutoring international students in English and went into her credential program knowing she wanted to work with international students, whether in the United States or abroad. This helped her solidify her career choice and gave her much-needed and hard-to-gain experience working with a select group of people.

Traveling and studying abroad can do a lot for your personal and professional growth. It is a great way to learn a new language, especially important if that language is needed for your new career. Other ways traveling and studying abroad can help you:

1. While you are abroad you can travel even more on the weekends—a great opportunity to see even more of a culture and meet different people.

2. Going to another country also gives you an opportunity to develop skills that you will never get in a classroom setting. You will be presented with new problems and challenges that

you will have to work through and then be so proud of yourself when you've accomplish it. These result in great stories for your interviews and are wonderful self-confidence builders.

3. You will grow your international network. We have a whole chapter for this later, but how great would it be to have international contacts? This has the "cool factor," if nothing else.

4. Traveling gets you out of your normal routine. It can be great for you to have a different perspective, experience different settings, and then return to the normal with a fresh set of eyes and a rejuvenated point of view.

5. Traveling abroad shows you are willing to face challenges and can give you opportunities you may not have otherwise had. Employers love anything that makes a job candidate different, so this can be a great chance to stand out and show you are willing to take the extra step to enhance your employment opportunities.

6. Studying internationally can enhance your degree. You will get the chance to take courses that you would never be able to take at your home campus, and you can learn things from a different perspective.

Many of the same rules apply here as they do to domestic traveling. Make the travel work for you. Use your time and relationships with people abroad to work for your résumé. If you have always wanted to go to France, take a study abroad trip and use the experience for your benefit in interviews with potential employers. Let them know what you picked up overseas that other applicants won't have.

NOTE: Don't just travel for the sake of traveling. Please make sure you have a good reason for leaving your network and all the momentum you've created for your career. Don't just go to hang out with your family and work at a minimum-wage retail position. Have an internship set up, or find a way to increase your business network to this area. (And feel free to also have that retail job if it will help financially support your internship and career path.) Remember to keep that momentum going by finding a way to make everything you do work for your résumé. Employers will look at the time line of your résumé (which we will cover later), and if you have random gaps they may doubt your commitment or wonder what caused you to halt your career trajectory. Make sure you are always working on something that will help you toward your career goals.

A Story

Lindsey, a current college student, believes that studying abroad in Ireland completely changed her life and outlook on her own career. She sat in her professor's office as a transfer student who already felt behind in her major and almost didn't go abroad because she didn't want to delay graduation. Then Lindsey spoke with her advisor and figured out that going to Ireland would not put her behind. After traveling abroad she became more independent, confident, and adaptable, and she believes she has a huge advantage in the job market. Lindsey has set herself apart from other college graduates in a way not many others have, and future employers are constantly looking for small ways that applicants are unique from others. She aspires to work for a company with an international presence and definitely sees her experience abroad as a key part of that desire.

Create Your Own Project

A great way to show your initiative and creativity is to create your own project. This can be done in many ways, and the more your project involves collaboration, the less you'll have to do all by yourself and the larger the project scope becomes. Don't worry about getting paid here, because it's all about the experience and showing off what you do best.

A Story

Lucerito, a Latina honors student, was so grateful for her education that she wanted to dedicate herself to encouraging other Latinos to finish their degrees. She decided to put on an event called Motivate! Discover Your Passion for Success. Once Lucerito began working on the event, it became clear that she needed more resources. So she started a student club, the Society of Latino Motivators, and through the club not only created a team of "assistants" to put on the event but also gained funding that was only available through officially recognized student organizations. The event drew six hundred people from throughout the area and at the end of the school year was granted awards and kudos from top administration officials. Lucerito's tremendous innovation at all levels of the project was a big part of the reason that she eventually became her college's Dean's Medalist.

Another Story

Eric loved his major so much that he was almost evangelical about it. He would sing its praises to anyone who would listen. One day he stopped by Professor Hays's office and said that he wanted to help recruit for the department. She told him that would be great, and they put together a plan for an ambassadors program. Eric recruited a team to help create a PowerPoint presentation, a powerful video, and handouts to use during talks at local high schools. He and his team pitched to the high schools and, as a result, gave many presentations to potential incoming students. Eric helped his major department and created something wonderful for his résumé that helped him land a job in event management shortly after graduation.

Find New Ways of Doing Things

A great way to excel inside and outside the classroom is to find new ways to do things. Be innovative! Identify something that your boss or professor does every day that you think could be done in a much better way. Such innovative insights usually come much more easily to people who are new to the situations and have fresh perspectives.

A Story

At one of my first internships at a nonprofit organization, they printed all of the media articles they were mentioned in every month and made thirty-plus copies of these packets for each of their board members. As you can imagine, each month the project created a stack of paper about two feet high. It was not only time consuming (and as the person who had to copy all of it I found it annoying) but also a huge waste of paper, as it was usually just tossed out by the board members. Out of frustration I decided to talk to our tech/web administration and found a way to scan them and put all the articles online, organized by month. The board members then had access to everything whenever they needed it. Aside from saving the organization a lot of money annually, this change also saved a lot trees and me a lot of headaches! I was able to put it on my résumé and felt really great about helping out. In addition, the organization was able to use this online archive as proof of its validity and excellent track record with the media. Innovation = a win for all!

Take a good look at what you do every day in your classes and at your job. Try to make a list of things that seem to take more time than they should. Reexamine the situation and see if there is a way that you can conquer the project or item more effectively. You will strengthen your innovation muscles and enhance your credibility with and value to those involved.

> Tɪᴘ: Whether you are interning or an employee, if you start to feel bored or dissatisfied with your work, be proactive and try to fix it. Find the things about your job that you do enjoy and innovate more around those tasks or projects. Find ways that you can develop enjoyable tasks and make your job more fun. Then tell your boss that you prefer those projects, and show him or her why it's important you work on those specific tasks. For example, if you love to write copy, experiment with different types of ads or social networking stories (like on Facebook) that you can write, and then show the impact these have on your company. If you independently find something that benefits your boss, then your boss will love you and you'll love what you do! Another way to beat boredom is to learn a new set of skills. Every boss loves an employee who wants to learn and become more valuable. And being more valuable is more important than ever in this job market. Volunteer to be the one to come up to speed on a new technology or client or vendor or customer. (Experts rarely get fired or laid off. Think of this idea as insurance.)

Cheat Sheet

- Start a business.
  - Create a business plan.
  - Try project fees.
  - Consider the hassle tax.
  - Create necessary paperwork.
  - Remember you're the boss.

- Travel
  - Domestically:
    - Don't get intimidated.
  - Internationally:
    - Make it worth your time.

- Create your own projects.

- Find new ways of doing things.

ALLOW FOR WIGGLE ROOM AND CELEBRATION
Professor Hays

In our hectic, usually overscheduled existences, we have practically eliminated the idea of wiggle room—those spaces in between appointments and deadlines where the beauty of life usually happens. Ironically, we are able to enjoy more success, and, frankly, more happiness, when we have less on our calendar for the day and when we build in what my first and all-time-favorite boss affectionately called *wiggle room*.

What Is Wiggle Room?

Perhaps the best way to define *wiggle room* is to describe what life looks like when you have some. When you have wiggle room:

- You don't feel rushed all the time.

- You aren't always late.

- You aren't constantly making excuses for things.

- You aren't consistently having this type of conversation with yourself: "Well, if I don't do this and this, I can still do this, and if I do this a little faster, I can still be on time."

- You look at your calendar and things are not scheduled back-to-back-to-back all day long.

- You accomplish your to-do list most days.

- You don't spend your entire day looking at a clock, watch, or other timekeeping device.

- You aren't annoyed when you have a chance encounter with a friend or acquaintance you haven't seen in a while that takes a few unexpected minutes. Instead, you enjoy the exchange, and it makes you happy all day.

- You regularly experience things that are not on your schedule—an impromptu conversation, a moment looking at a bird building a nest, an article that catches your eye.

When you have wiggle room, you have the option to linger a bit at the end of a class or meeting and have the conversations that really move things forward. You increase your meaningful networking by giving those with you your full attention. You enjoy lower blood pressure because you are not always stressed out and rushing. You breathe more deeply. You smile more.

Sound like an impossible fantasy? I used to think so too. But it isn't.

I can't guarantee that I can eliminate all of the stress in your life, but I can certainly help you get rid of most of it. Sound appealing? Read on . . .

An Aha Moment via a Forwarded E-mail

Something probably not unique about me is that I really don't like forwarded e-mails. You know, the jokes and the cute pictures of puppies and kitties and babies, as well as the ones that make you answer questions and send them on, and the ones that make you feel like your world will end and God will strike you down if you don't forward them to eight people in five minutes.

And, to be quite honest, I usually delete them without reading them (sorry, Mom). But for some reason a few years ago I read one, and it talked about having "margins." Being a writer, I immediately thought of page margins, but it wasn't talking about that. It was talking about this whole idea of wiggle room and how we should give ourselves spaces in our lives to set ourselves up for success. It reminded me that, if we are honest, we cause a lot of our own stress. Let me write that again just in case it didn't sink in the first time: *We cause a lot of our own stress.*

And, just like that, my plan for building more margins and wiggle room into my life was born, and now I am sharing that plan with you.

Quit Overscheduling

Lack of wiggle room is directly related to not having any space in our calendars. The best way to solve this problem is to quit overscheduling. Most days, your calendar should not be completely filled in. Some days it is impossible to avoid. Believe me, I know all about those days when we don't have a lot of control over our schedules, but when you can, have some spaces in between things. You can have an idea of what you would like to do in those spaces, but try to leave some looseness to your day so you can take advantage of things that come up unexpectedly. This could be personal, like going to a movie with that cute person in your chemistry lab, or professional, like an opportunity to hear a great speaker that you just heard about. If you are scheduled to the minute, you make it impossible to be spontaneous, and often it is these spontaneous moments that give your life its depth and joy and best opportunities.

Here are some tips for creating wiggle room:

- Say yes *only* to things you (1) absolutely need to do or (2) absolutely want to do *and* (3) have time to do. It is far worse to say yes and flake than to say no at the beginning. Memorize these phrases:
  - "Thank you for thinking of me, but I am not able to help at this time."
  - "Oh, that sounds like such fun, but I am already booked that day."
  - "While I am honored, I am afraid my plate is already full."

- Most polite people will not press you for details, but if you encounter some who do, memorize this phrase: "As you know, I am working toward becoming a [fill in your dream career], and I have so much to do to get there!" This will make the nosy folks feel bad (which you might agree is a good thing).

- Schedule study sessions, group project meetings, and everything else for twenty minutes or forty-five minutes instead of thirty and sixty. Most things can get accomplished in the shorter amount of time, and then you've got built-in wiggle room before the next thing. If things wrap up faster, you have even more wiggle room, and if they go a bit long, you are still okay.

- Use the phone instead of meeting in person. Even if you have to "meet" with more than one person, there are free conference-call companies out there so you can talk to several people at once at no charge. (FreeConferenceCall.com is one that I have had a lot of success with.) If you can meet on the phone, you save travel time and might even be able to multitask (dishes; driving—with a headset; folding laundry; etc.).

- Don't go immediately from school to work. As tempting as this may be, schedule some wiggle room between your school life and work. Even if it's thirty minutes to stay on campus, it will be worth it. You can study, wander, have a conversation, eat a snack, visit a professor, and so forth.

Stop the "One More Thing" Habit

Many of us suffer from I'll-just-do-one-more-thing-itis, meaning that we often try to write one more paragraph or one more e-mail, send one more text, post one more Tweet, or start one final to-do item right before leaving to go somewhere, thus causing frequent lateness and stress due to being rushed. If you have no idea what I'm talking about, you may move on to the next section. Still reading? I figured most of you would know exactly what I mean. The best way I have found to break the "I'll just do one more thing" habit is to work backward and use a timer.

How to work backward: Figure out what time you have to stop working on whatever it is you are working on, and move toward leaving. This is not as easy as it sounds, as you'll need to estimate how much time it will take to finish all of the last-minute items that you need to finish before you actually head out toward the next thing. You may even want to build in a few minutes to double-check the door locks, feed the dog, put on fresh lipstick, or whatever else might come up. When you are doing this analysis, build in the time it will take to arrive at your next thing comfortably, without being rushed. Account for normal walking time if you are walking and normal driving time if you are driving (without counting on speeding or hitting every green light). This will be a tough exercise for many of you. I know it was for me when I first started out. You will get better over time, though—I promise!

Then, set a timer that will let you know when that time has arrived. I much prefer timers over keeping track of time on a watch or clock or phone, because I believe that clock watching is (1) annoying and (2) not productive. I love the timer app I have on my phone, and I also use free online timers as well on my computer. When you set a timer, it does the work of keeping track of time for you, so you can focus on everything else. When the timer goes off, stop whatever you are doing, make a note of the next step or thought (if necessary), and move toward the door. If you really have a severe case of I'll-just-do-one-more-thing-itis, set your original timer for five fewer minutes, and when it goes off set it for five more minutes. This allows for those inevitable "I'm almost done" moments and last steps that you will need to take before actually transitioning toward leaving.

Do this more often than not, and you'll see magical wiggle room appear, your breathing will deepen, and smiles will come more easily.

Once you are in the habit of actually leaving when you should be leaving, in order to arrive at your destination comfortably and happily, you'll enjoy all of the things that you are doing more, as you won't arrive frazzled and stressed from trying to get there via an unrealistic time frame.

Yes, sometimes we do have to rush, as life is not 100 percent within our control. But before you start using this as an excuse, think about the last five times you arrived somewhere and felt a bit harried. Now think about whose fault it was that you felt that way. Was it yours? I thought so. And who has the ability to change the likelihood of feeling this way again? Yes, again it's all you. It's a choice, but it's one I encourage you to repeatedly make.

Choose Better Deadlines

As busy people, we also tend to put unnecessary stress on ourselves through assigning bad deadlines, both to ourselves and others. This definitely falls in with this chapter's theme that we often are the architects of our own stress because of a failure to build in wiggle room.

With ourselves, we sometimes look at an actual deadline—say, an assignment due date—and set our own deadline for completion extremely close to the actual deadline, leaving no room for wiggling (i.e., dealing with anything unexpected). When we do this, and then our printer runs out of ink, or we need to get gas in the car before we go to class, or something else comes up at the last minute, we miss deadlines that we really should have met. We certainly could have met them, but we assigned ourselves a bad deadline.

The solution? Give yourself a good deadline—one that allows you to accomplish the task at hand and builds in a little wiggle room to allow for the unexpected, or the opportunity to go on an impromptu ice-cream run or dog walk.

But a word of caution: Setting good deadlines is not the same as doing everything the minute a task is assigned and putting nothing off, ever, even for a day or so—even if it is appropriate or okay.

A Story

I had a colleague who did everything the minute it was assigned, and as such he always had things done well before actual deadlines, but he didn't have much of a life either. He worked sunrise to sundown and most weekends. It was not unusual at all to get e-mails from him at 5 A.M. and also at 10 P.M. He returned all texts and e-mails almost immediately. I often thought that if he set his deadlines more appropriately, doing the most pressing items first and assigning good deadlines to the others, he would have had more time to do things other than work.

There will always be more things to do than there is time to do them, so this "when you are going to do what" process is important. Remember your Priorities Right Now list, take care of that first, set your personal deadlines with built-in wiggle room for the rest, and you'll be just fine.

When we assign deadlines to others, we can also create stress for ourselves. Sometimes we want to be nice and give people all the time that they can physically have in order to get something done. For example, if someone is doing the writing and you are the editor and the finished assignment is due at 2 P.M., you might be tempted to give your work partner until 1 P.M. or even 1:30 P.M. to write, knowing that the editing "shouldn't" take more than thirty minutes to complete. See the problem here? You have built in no wiggle room for you to accomplish your part of the project should something come up on your end or should your piece take longer than you have anticipated. You have also not allowed at all for your work partner to miss or be late with his or her deadline and still have everything be okay. People miss deadlines and are late with things all the time—and since you cannot control others, it's best to build in time for them to do what humans sometimes do and still not harm your chances for success. A better idea would be to give your work partner a deadline of 10 A.M., allowing plenty of wiggle room for him to take extra time if necessary and plenty of wiggle room for you being able to edit and make your 2 P.M. deadline. Better yet, give him the deadline of 8 A.M. or even the night before.

Bottom line: When you think about it, you have a lot of control over when you need to do most of the things that you have to do. You might not have set the final deadline for your assignments or projects, but you can set the deadlines that lead to their completion. You can do this in one of two ways—with wiggle room or without. Choose wisely.

A Story

When Tori and I were writing this book last May, we had a September 28 deadline for completion of the manuscript. Both of us were going to be very busy in the month of May (me with graduation and Tori with a big work deadline), so we chose not to have any deadlines that month in anticipation of not being able to realistically meet them. We also knew that September was to be extremely booked for both of us (me with back-to-school for my job and my children and Tori with her upcoming wedding), so we wanted to try to be done before then. Come June 1, we met via Skype and worked out a schedule. Every two weeks we had a deadline for a piece of the book, and we would hold each other accountable via biweekly meetings. If we were to follow this schedule to the letter, we would have been done with the manuscript by August 15, well before our actual deadline and well before our self-imposed deadline of August 31. This plan gave us two weeks of wiggle room for our own ideal deadline and six weeks of wiggle room prior to the real deadline imposed by the publisher. (We also didn't tell our publisher that we were planning on being so early, just in case we needed the wiggle room we had given ourselves.) Working this way kept us on track, but we were never worried or stressed if we were a few hundred words short on a chapter prior to one of our biweekly check-ins or if it was taking a bit longer than planned to write our author bios. We moved along fairly well until late July, when things were busier than we had both anticipated. Because of our built-in wiggle room, however, we were able to finish on time and turn our manuscript in by our actual deadline. Everyone was happy because we gave ourselves good deadlines. This story, of course, could've turned out much differently if we had chosen to set bad deadlines, or even fewer deadlines.

Build In Spaces Daily to Breathe

Ah, breathing. It's so underrated, especially by college students. Part of having wiggle room is to build in breathing room to each day. Frankly, building in time to breathe each hour would be nirvana (the state of mind, not the rock group of my youth!), but this might be an unrealistic goal for many.

But you are so busy, right? You have no time to breathe or sleep or any of that, correct? Well, let's, again, be honest with ourselves. Is that really true? Are you really *so* busy that you can't breathe? It sounds absurd when you pause and think about it, doesn't it?

Granted, sometimes you *are* that busy—perhaps during the week of final exams or the winter holiday season or maybe a busy period at your job or internship. If that's the case, fine. Power through it, and we'll catch up with you on the other side. For the most part, however, we can all take time to breathe. Please note, however, that, like actually holding your breath, powering through it can only be your plan of attack for so long. At some point you are going to *have* to take a breather, or your body will force you to (probably by getting sick, and no one wants that!).

Once again I'm going to sing the praises of my timer. I use it all the time, as described above, for letting me know when I need to get ready to go to the next thing. But I also use it when I have nowhere to go and I'll be sitting at my computer for an extended length of time. When I sit down, I first assess my energy level, my attention span, and the work I have to do. Working my to-do-list from most important to least, I decide what my time blocks are going to be. Usually they are thirty to forty-five minutes, but some days they are twenty-five or even twenty, and some days fifteen. I set the timer, work like crazy for that set amount of time, and then, when the timer goes off, get up and walk around. Then I breathe and maybe do a few simple stretches. (Confession: Sometimes I don't get up, and I just reset the timer and keep working, but I never allow myself to set it for a third time without getting up). Then I go back to the computer, reset the timer, and get back to work. Usually this is when I set the timer for ten minutes or so to catch up on e-mail so I am in the loop on things but e-mail doesn't suck all of my time or energy away from what I have determined I should be doing. Once that timer goes off, I set it for the bigger chunk of time, and I keep going . . . working, breathing, e-mail, working, breathing, and so on . . . until it's time to get up and go somewhere else.

Get Up Earlier

Another idea to secure more time to breathe (and thus more wiggle room) is to get up earlier. Yeah, I know, getting up early is tough. I am not by nature a morning person, and growing up that adage "the early bird gets the worm" wasn't very motivating, as I've always thought worms were gross and didn't ever want to get one, especially if that meant I had to get out of bed to do it. (In fact, my mother still hasn't forgiven me for sleeping in instead of going with her to see the Olympic torch go by in 1984.) But, as I do the math between the number of hours in a day and the number of things on my to-do list, it all adds up to an early wake-up time, especially if I want to have any wiggle room at all.

Mornings are notoriously absent of wiggle room for most of us, all of which can be avoided with a few less taps to the snooze button. Again, think about this, even for just a minute, and you know I am right. If you still aren't sold, try to think of a time when you weren't rushing out the door. Felt good, right? And if you can't think of a time when you weren't rushing out the door, you need this idea more than most.

Start small or start big, depending on your personality and tolerance for alarm clocks. Even an extra ten or fifteen minutes can make a big difference when trying to create morning wiggle room.

One summer a few years ago I realized that I probably could accomplish all of my life's goals if I would consistently get up at 5:30 A.M. I'm still not there (usually I am out of bed by 6:15 A.M.), and, subsequently, there are several important goals that I have yet to accomplish. I believe there is a definite and concrete connection between those two truths.

More about Punctuality

As we discussed in chapter 2, being punctual is one of the best things you can do to build your brand. Interestingly, being punctual is also one of the best things you can do to build wiggle room into your day. When you consistently arrive a few minutes early—again, four minutes is plenty—you'll be able to review your goals for the class or appointment or meeting (as discussed in chapter 5) and you'll be in the proper frame of mind to get what you want out of the time.

This, of course, is in addition to the wonderful happy feeling you will have because you didn't have to break traffic laws to arrive at your destination.

And you'll always have time to take a big, deep, beautiful breath (or two!) before things get rolling.

Procrastination as It Relates to Wiggle Room

This may go without saying, but I feel I need to say (or write) it anyway. Obviously, procrastination is the enemy of wiggle room. Things put off and things done at the last minute, by definition, do not contain wiggle room. If you weren't sold on the value of not procrastinating in chapter 4, perhaps you will be now. If you'd like, go ahead and review the "kill the procrastination bug" sections again in chapter 4 to really get you motivated. Quick summary—break ugly tasks into manageable chunks, do them as early in the day as you can, and perhaps even reward yourself for doing them.

A Story

A great wiggle-room success story actually happened during the writing of this chapter. I had blocked out most of a whole day to get started on this section, as I had scheduled an early morning coffee with a professional acquaintance who wanted to brainstorm ways to learn a little more about a particular industry in order to build her freelance business. I had a full day of writing to do, but since I had planned on beginning my writing in the same coffee shop after our meeting, I did not have to race off to my next appointment. We had a lovely visit, shared a lot of information, and at the very end talked a little about this book, a topic not on our discussion agenda. Well, this woman is also the producer of a local radio news program, and, as she was leaving, she offered me our first media interview after the book was published! In my heart I knew that this would not have happened if I hadn't built wiggle room into my day. I hadn't scheduled myself to the minute and therefore allowed something beautiful and beneficial to happen.

An hour later, as I sat there fueled up on delicious coffee, typing away, into the coffee shop walked an acquaintance I hadn't seen in years. We are friends on Facebook, so I know what's going on in her world, but there is no substitute for face-to-face connection. I was able to happily greet her because I had wiggle room in my day and not get caught looking at my watch wondering when she would be leaving. This woman was someone I had thought about pitching for a workshop, and now I had the perfect excuse to circle back with an e-mail without it sounding completely out of the blue. You see, money can even be made via wiggle room.

Include Celebration

One of the best uses of your newfound wiggle room is the infusion of more celebration. Successes, as we all know, are not easy to come by. Ironically, once we do get them we often just move onto the next thing with barely a "woo hoo" or knuckle touch. Now, I am not bashing on the merits of a solidly placed knuckle touch or the joy that comes from an extremely loud "woo hoo." My point is that your new celebration lifestyle should encompass more than that. Proper and frequent acknowledgment of successes leads to more of them.

A Story

When I first started my career I worked for a small PR firm in Sacramento that had an amazing corporate culture that believed in celebrating wins. It was tradition that when there was something to celebrate, we did, with champagne in the conference room, usually at 4 or 4:30 P.M. In the early days, we'd simply shout across the office, as we were close to each other and there weren't that many of us. And later, when we were bigger and on two floors, we'd get an e-mail with the announcement. We always celebrated big wins, like new clients or successful media events, but we also celebrated small things, like a new fax machine or someone making a tough deadline or a solid compliment from a client. The important thing was to stop and mark the moment as significant and worthy of celebration. On rare occasions, we even celebrated for no particular reason, which is also good practice.

We would always take the champagne cork and write on it the reason for our celebration—and then we'd throw the cork up on the top of this credenza, out of site of clients and visitors. A few years after I left the firm, I heard from the partners that they were getting ready to celebrate an important milestone and wanted me to be there for the celebration. And even though I didn't even live in California anymore, they flew me out and put me up in a hotel to make sure I could attend. At the party they gave each of us a small Plexiglas pyramid with a cork inside, one that represented that particular employee.

Excitedly, I looked at mine.

It said, "No reason in particular."

At first I was insulted, thinking they couldn't remember anything good I'd ever done for them, but then they explained that I received that cork because of my ability to embrace their idea of celebration. And while that party was almost twenty years ago, I still have my cork and I still try to practice the idea of celebrating wins—as many as I can.

Celebrate All Wins

Most people get the idea of celebrating big wins—Super Bowl or World Series victories, landing a huge client, turning twenty-one (or forty)—but most don't regularly (or irregularly) celebrate the small wins that add up to the big ones.

Even if it's just a pause at a staff meeting, or during a meal, to raise a glass or give a shout-out, do it. And do it often. Many, many great things will come of the practice. Here are some ideas:

- Cheers daily at dinner.
  - If you eat dinner with others, ask them to name the best thing about their day. If they say, "Nothing," then prod a little more. Eventually they will give something up. You can even make the conversation deeper by having rules. My daughter, for example, won't allow me to mention anything food related as the best part of my day. Evidently what I had for lunch topped my list a few too many times!
  - Offer frequent toasts. Raise your glass on a regular basis with a "Cheers to the cooler temperatures today!" or "Cheers to flip-flops!" or "Cheers to [whatever has made you happy that day]!"

- Share often with others.
  - Forward a nice note from your boss to your professor, or a note from your professor to your boss, and both to your parents. If you are uncomfortable with this, just add a note that says, "Wow, isn't this so nice?" or something else that sounds humble.

- Give kudos liberally and frequently.
  - Regularly send e-mails or post on Facebook or Twitter about the good things that others do. "Great job, [name], on the presentation in class today." Or "Wow, congrats, [name], on your new internship. They are lucky to have you!" Shining the light on others only shines right back on you, and *everyone* likes to be acknowledged for their good work.

- Schedule monthly celebration time.
  - Make a regular date with friends, family, or whomever you'd like to toast and celebrate the great things that have happened during the last month. You could make it like a club, where the only requirement for membership is a good

    attitude and a mandatory declaration each month of something good.

- ○ NOTE: Not everyone will enjoy or be comfortable with this club, so don't feel bad if you get folks who decline your invitation. Hopefully they'll join you later as they want some of your "secret sauce" for life!
- ○ This idea is good practice for making good choices regarding whom to allow in your life. As you move forward, you won't have time for everyone, and you'll need to become more selective about the people you spend your time with. If you choose people who, like you, would rather celebrate life than complain about it, all the good stuff will keep perpetuating itself.

Celebrate the Steps So You Don't Live Exclusively in the Future

Especially when you are in college, life seems a lot about preparation. You take one course in order to prepare for the next. You complete an internship in order to be able to apply for the next one. You are earning your degree and reading this book in order to land your dream career. This is all important, but what is also important is employing enough mindfulness to not be living in the future.

The steps toward your success need to also be celebrated. Two main reasons: (1) celebration of success leads to the celebration of more success and (2) celebrating steps helps you stay in the present and enjoy your life *now*.

I have students come in for advising all the time who are focused on one thing—getting out of college as fast as they can. And while financial considerations certainly play into this way of thinking, I often take the opportunity to remind them that this isn't a race. When class schedules or life prevent a student from graduating "on time" and require staying an extra semester, he or she is often very upset, and usually it's because they had an artificial deadline set up without any real meaning. I then remind them that *no one* will ever ask you how long it took for you to graduate from college. All that needs to be on your résumé is the end date, which is what future employers care about. If you choose to tell people it took you four and a half—or five, or even seven—years, that's your business, but rarely will people ask. The point here is that you shouldn't rush through college (mentally or physically). Enjoy it. It is fun. It is exciting. And it's the only time like this you'll ever have. You'll never be an undergraduate again, so soak it up.

Remind Yourself to Embrace Joy

Let's talk a little more about enjoying your life *now*.

Let's face it, life is often difficult. And, if you wanted to, you could find enough bad news each day to allow yourself to become deeply depressed. You could easily spend all day dwelling on things that make you unhappy, people you don't like, and things that you are worried about. You might know people who choose to live their lives that way. Conversely, if you look, you can also find enough each day to fill your heart with gratitude and be happy to be alive. I think you can guess which choice is a better life strategy.

For example, during a particular day you could wake up and stub your toe, and I mean stub it *really* hard on your dresser. Then you could drive to school and get the perfect parking spot and then have no line at the sandwich place at lunch. And then you could really enjoy your classes and maybe even get out of one a few minutes early. On the way home, you could get a call letting you know that you have an interview for an internship that you really want. When you come home, your roommate could ask you how your day was, and you might answer, "Oh, my gosh, I stubbed my toe so bad this morning. Look, it's still red!" You know people like this, and sometimes even you might be like this. Clearly when you read this it seems ridiculous, but humans tend to focus on the negative more often than the good.

This doesn't have to be you.

You can choose to live a life—personally and professionally—of celebrating wins.

Cheat Sheet

- We all need wiggle room.

- Quit overscheduling.
  - Have twenty- or forty-five-minute meetings.
  - Say yes *only* to things you (1) absolutely need to do or (2) absolutely want to do *and* (3) have time to do.

- Stop the "one more thing" habit.
  - Work backward and set a timer.

- Choose better deadlines—for yourself and others.

- Build in spaces daily to breathe.
  - Get up earlier.

- Renew your commitment to punctuality.

- Don't procrastinate.

- Include celebration.
  - Celebrate all wins.
  - Cheers daily at dinner.
  - Share often with others.
  - Give kudos liberally and frequently.
  - Schedule monthly celebration time.
  - Celebrate the steps so you don't live in the future.
  - Remind yourself to embrace joy.

CHAPTER EIGHT
NETWORK, NETWORK, NETWORK
Tori

I f you've taken any career courses or gone to any career fairs, undoubtedly you've had this word thrown at you: *network.* By now you should
know it's important, and whether you are aware or not, networking
is part of your daily life. Every time you sign onto Facebook, Twitter,
Pinterest, or Instagram you are networking. You are sharing interests and
engaging and communicating with others. In fact, you are the generation
of networking. You were born and bred to do it. But what does it mean,
really, to network professionally?

Networking means to increase the amount of people in your circle, or
circles. Grow your resources, mentors, guides, referrals, references, and
even friends. With each person you add to your personal network, you
increase potential career opportunities tenfold.

A Story

Have you ever heard of six degrees of separation? It is the belief
that any person can find a personal introduction to any other
person in the world through six people. The entrepreneurship
program at my university wanted to experiment with this concept.
They told each student in the program to think of a very influential
person who could greatly impact their career path. Once they had
picked this person, they were then told that they had to find an
introduction to that person through their network in six steps. One
of the students I knew picked Donald Trump. Tough pick, right? All
the students in the program began to network tirelessly to get to

131

that one person, and most, if not all, succeeded. Even the one who chose Donald Trump! (In fact, it only took her two steps to get to him; what a network!)

The point of this chapter isn't to introduce you to Donald Trump (bummer!), but it is to make sure that you understand what networking is, why to do it, who to do it with, where and when it is appropriate, and ultimately how to get the most out of it.

Why Network?

What you just read really should answer this question, but if you need more clarification—*networking can get you a job*! And not just a job at a fast food joint, but the job that could be what you love or the stepping-stone to the career of your dreams. And once you have that dream job, your network can continue to nurture you and help you grow, as long as you keep putting your time and energy back into it.

Networking also goes far beyond your career. Your network can be a wonderful sounding board for you in any area of your life. Not sure which class you should take? Reach out to someone you trust in your network for advice. Want to learn something new in your industry? Call someone who knows more than you do to help you get through it. Ultimately, through your network you should gain wisdom, new ideas, and new perspectives. Your network should not only help you succeed but also develop you as a person. You should be able to reach into your network and come out smarter and better than you would have been on your own.

Your network is also your safety net. When you have too much on your plate, your network can be a wonderful resource to help you prioritize, say no, or even get it done. When you have a personal need, such as a ride somewhere or a recommendation for a mechanic when your car breaks down, reach out to your network. I promise, you can't do everything on your own!

When you lose a job, your network can be a great resource for you via encouraging, helping, and even potentially saving you with the connection for the perfect job. I, like many others in this down economy, have been laid off—twice, actually, early on in my career. This could have devastated me, turned my world upside down, and forced me to lose hope in everything I had worked so hard to achieve. And I'll be honest, I definitely cried a lot. Luckily, I have an amazing network that has saved me more than once, providing contacts and introductions that led me to be gainfully employed in virtually no time at all. Most recently, I was only out of work for twenty-six hours.

A Story (Actually Two Stories)

The first time I was laid off I had been working for a nonprofit, and they simply didn't have the funds to continue paying me. I was completely shocked; I had never expected to be laid off—ever! I was an extremely hard worker and very close to everyone I worked with. Walking out of the building, I couldn't believe what had happened. Looking back, this was a turning point in my life. I went home, refreshed my résumé, got a letter of recommendation from my last boss, and reached out to my network. Within a week, I had an interview with someone who had spoken at a networking event I had attended a few months prior. He hired me as an intern, then promoted me to manage all of his interns, and ultimately gave me my first out-of-college job. At graduation I was one of few with a full-time paid position, and it felt really good. I could have never done it on my own, though, and it took a lot of encouragement from my network, as well as the job connections to get me through it.

The second time I was laid off was from a real-world job, and it was sudden. I received a call that I was laid off as of 5 P.M. that day—with no extra pay or anything. I had also just heard that my car needed about $1,200 worth of repairs, and I lived on my own in a high-rent, twelve-month-lease apartment. All I could think was, *How am I going to make this work?* Okay, I'll admit it: I cried again. But I think this is the best story of how intricate and amazing my network is. I immediately went home, applied for unemployment, refreshed my personal website and résumé, and e-mailed key people in my network. At the time I was coaching cheerleading part time in the afternoons, and I decided to go because being around the kids would make me feel better. While at cheer practice, a parent noticed I was "a little off" and asked our head coach what was wrong. The coach, who also happened to be my mom, explained

133

what had happened, and the cheer mom told her to have me call her in the morning. This woman was the CEO of a tech start-up and needed my help. I called her the next morning and had a job by that afternoon. That's right—I had a twenty-six-hour job search. And through the next week, I had several other job opportunities come through from my network that could have also been a great way for me to make it through. In a horrible economy where I had friends who had been looking for jobs for more than a year, I still can't believe how lucky and blessed I was to have a network that made these wonderful stories possible.

Who Should Be in Your Network?

Everybody! And I seriously mean every person you run into. You never know who could potentially be the best asset for your growing network. Think that you don't need to pay attention to that shoe shiner or the receptionist at an office? They may have the best network out of anyone in the building.

Just think: The executives of a company in a building that has a shoe shiner probably like to get their shoes shined and in doing so have conversations with the shoe shiner. If you are friendly and really get to know that person, no strings attached, just showing him or her that you are genuinely interested in getting to know and helping him or her, that shoe shiner might just have the "in" that you need. Mentioning you in their next session with the executive might be the boost you need.

Same with the receptionist: Think they're not important? Think again. A receptionist is a business's gatekeeper. They can make or break you with anyone in their office. If there is a hole in someone's schedule that you want to squeeze into, the number one person to have on your side is the keeper of schedules—a.k.a. the receptionist. They also have great networks within the company and can introduce you to pretty much anyone. Keep this in mind any time you go into a building and put your game face, best smile, and personality on.

This also goes beyond your workplace. When you go to your favorite restaurant, get to know the people. Maybe the bartender has a friend or uncle who works for a company you're interested in, and just a quick text later you have an informational interview with a person of influence.

Your family is also a great resource. Now, it may or may not be a good idea to go into business with your family members or even work for them, but their networks and decades of wisdom can be wonderful resources for you. In fact, I got my first real corporate job/internship through my uncle with his company. And then I got to carpool with him and have lunch with him, although we worked in completely separate departments.

The point here is to realize that you can't do it alone. You can't know everything or do it all. You may have heard the phrase, "It's not what you know, it's who you know." This is very true. Employers will want you to have references, and anyone you can put on that page that they already trust in their network is a *huge* win for you.

A Story

When my husband and I bought our house, the housing market in our area was awful. We spent months looking and putting in offers tens of thousands of dollars over asking prices. Our realtor was wonderful and supportive, but everyone was having the same problems, and most realtors were encouraging buyers to step out of the market, save more, and return when it had calmed down a bit. We were determined to not give up. Our realtor persuaded us to look at a house because the selling realtor was in her network and she knew he would give our offer serious consideration because of her rapport with him. And guess what? Even with several other offers vying for their attention, we got the house! I had never been influenced so directly by someone else's network, but I definitely was happy.

Since then I have paid attention to our realtor, who also happens to be a great family friend, and I have learned several things about networking. First, and very important, she knows just about *everyone*, as she is always talking to people everywhere we go. And if she doesn't know them personally, she finds a personal connection to them, through however many steps it takes. She continues to amaze me as an excellent example of a person who networks with everyone everywhere she goes.

When Should You Network?

Let's see, can you guess? Always! Just like the last story, make it your mission to talk and find a connection with at least one person everywhere you go. You'd be amazed the connections you can find with people.

You should know by now that there aren't any downtimes for networking and that you never know which connection or person on the street could lead to your next big break. You should always have your brand ready as well as your elevator pitches (chapter 5) prepped to go when you meet anyone.

Knowing when to network also means reading people. If someone is in a bad mood or you've caught them off guard, it's probably not the best time to hand them a business card. You want people to be in the best frame of mind when you are asking them for something, and trying to become part of their network is asking them for something—their attention and interest. You want them to want to help you as much as you promise you can help them (remember, it is a two-way street). So if they seem to be down, irritated, or angry and you can't pull them out of it with the best smile you've got, hold off and approach them another time. I'm sure you can create another opportunity to meet them.

Use Your Student Status

Perhaps the most important part of the when-to-network question, however, is to do it now while you're still a student. As we've mentioned previously—actually several times, because it is such a critical piece to all of this—when you're a student you are practically invincible in the world of networking. Professionals for the most part want to see you succeed and don't feel any pressure to talk to you because you don't need a job from them (not yet, anyway).

You definitely want to use your student status while you can, and one of the best ways to do this is through informational interviews. We've mentioned this a few times throughout this book, and here is where we will break it down. An informational interview is when you find someone through your network, or even via a cold call, and ask them if they would mind telling you how they landed the job they have now—the job of your dreams!

What do you do in an informational interview? Take the opportunity to listen and learn from someone who has been in your industry and has been very successful. Here's what to bring: a list of questions, your résumé and portfolio (if you have one), and a great attitude. The résumé and portfolio are just in case they are interested enough to ask how your progress is going, but make sure they ask before you break it out. And if you don't have a portfolio yet, don't let it stop you, as you should really start doing informational interviews the second you finish this chapter. Don't wait! You'll probably be shocked by how many questions people end up asking you and how interested folks get in your desired career path.

Tip: Go see them in person. Why? You show the person you're interviewing you're serious because you've put the effort into driving and dressing up for the occasion. You can show off a lot more of your personality by seeing them in person and not being worried about technology failures or issues. If you have a portfolio of your work, you can bring it with you and get their opinions. You can also meet others in their office easily and build your network more than you might have expected. Also, you can get a feel for their work environment, which is really significant. You'll start to learn which sized workplaces make you feel comfortable, which types of workspaces you think you'd enjoy, and which areas of town you'd like the best. While what you actually do on the job is key, of course, to career satisfaction, the work environment does count as well. Trust me, I wish I did this more while still a student.

Sample questions to take to an informational interview:

1. "Why did you decide this was the career for you? When did you decide to enter this career? Was this always what you wanted to do when you grew up?"

2. "What did you study that led you to this career? What classes helped the most, and, on a daily basis, what impacts you most from what you learned?"

3. "What led you to your current position?"

4. "What does a typical day look like for you?" [You might want to use "air quotes" when you say the word *typical*, as most professionals laugh at the idea of a typical day, but they know what you mean.]

5. "What do you love most about your job?"

6. "If you could change one thing about it, what would it be?"

7. "If you could go back and give yourself one piece of advice when you were still in college, what would it be?"

8. "What do you look for when you are hiring?" [This is a great opportunity for you to take meticulous notes, especially if you want to work here one day.]

9. "Do you have a specific time your company likes to hire college graduates?" [Very important for your senior year to know when to reach back out to them and apply. If you know the date, you could be one of the first applications in!]

10. "Do you have an intern program? If so, what does the out-of-school hire rate look like from that pool of interns?"

11. "Do you have anyone else you would recommend I talk to, at this company or another?"

12. "Anything else you would like to add?"

13. *Say thank you.*

Number 11 is critical, as it helps your network continue to grow. The great news is that, especially if you've had an enjoyable conversation, the person you are meeting with is only going to give you quality pros to talk to. They aren't going to look in their contact list for all the jerks; that just doesn't make sense. Always leave each informational interview with a few people to contact, and then soon you'll have too many and will need to prioritize. What a great problem to have! To help prioritize, give yourself some numerical goals. Try for a certain number of informational interviews each semester and during each school break. Then you'll know how many you can stack up and decide as you go if some are worth more than others.

During the interview, be sure to take diligent notes. You can't be expected to remember every detail, but the more you can bring up later when you reconnect the better. It will also help you build your database, because they might tell you different places that they've worked and connections that they have that you could possibly take advantage of later. If the person you are interviewing is comfortable, you could also record your interview and pull out the useful bits later. That way you can really pay attention, read their face, and look engaged in the conversation.

After the informational interview, make sure you follow up. Send a thank you note, and keep them updated on your progress. Remember, if a student calls and asks how a professional got his or her job, inquires about a typical day, or needs mentoring or help, the student is much more likely to receive help than a college graduate would. It bears repeating: After graduating, students are considered grown up and are expected to fend for themselves.

A Story

When I was still in college, I had a "freak-out moment" when I realized I wanted to move to a different part of the state when I graduated and I didn't want to move home with my parents, which meant I needed a (well-paying) job. I conducted a few informational interviews with people in the area where I wanted to move, asking many of the questions above, and learned a lot, greatly increasing my network with each new person I talked to. Everyone I interviewed was extremely friendly and helpful and ended up asking me a lot about myself, including what I had done up to that point in my life and what my plans were. I received some internship opportunities then, but what amazes me is that I still (a few years later) hear from those I had early informational interviews with regarding possible job opportunities.

Take Advantage of Your Limited-Time Audience

Another great reason to network while you're still a student is because you are surrounded by a vast amount of people who are also interested in growing their networks.

139

Think of it this way: Let's say you want to meet the perfect guy or girl. College is an excellent place to meet the perfect mate. Many campuses have thousands of students, all with different backgrounds, interests, and characteristics for you to pick from. But once you graduate you don't have that same easy access to this vast peer group, so many resort to bars or online dating, which are much more awkward and difficult ways to cultivate a relationship.

The same rings true for professional relationships: Once you graduate from college there are far fewer ways to meet other similarly interested professionals in the real world. You generally meet new people at work, through a professional association, or online through sites like Facebook or LinkedIn (which we'll talk more about in chapter 9).

So what's the lesson? Use this limited time in college to your professional advantage. This is one of the pieces of advice I would drill into you again and again from this book: You're only a student for a limited time, so use it to your advantage!

Where Should You Network?

Everywhere

And I literally mean everywhere. Anywhere you are where there are people, you should be bragging (gracefully) about yourself and letting your brand be known. This includes, but is not limited to, networking events, job fairs, conferences, classes, meetings, lunches, and online.

I'll go into a few areas in a little more detail.

Meetings

Whether you are working as a volunteer, intern, or employee, network with those you work with every time you sit down for a meeting. This may seem a bit odd, because generally you are in meetings with people you already know. But sometimes we don't take advantage of these precious moments. Make it a mission to learn something new about each person you work with every time you meet with them. You might be surprised to find out new things that you never knew about someone you work with. This could give you a much better connection and lead to better, deeper conversations as well as an easier way to maintain and grow your relationship.

Many times you will also meet with people outside of your company. I have conference calls at least weekly, and I cannot tell you how many times I get on a call with someone I've never talked to before and these three same questions are asked:

1. "How are you?"

2. "Where are you based?"/"Where do you work?"

3. "How's the weather there?"

Really? Is that the best we can do? Take advantage of these people coming into your network and make sure they know who you are. Use those brand points, elevator pitches, and the stories you created earlier in this book to have a memorable and enjoyable conversation with these new people. Get to know what their wants and needs are. It doesn't take long, I promise. A simple "I'm doing great! I've been working on cooking gluten-free at home, and while it's been a struggle because I've never been the best chef, I'm a pretty determined person, and it will take a lot of bad cupcakes to derail me. My officemates, on the other hand, might start revolting from the experiments I bring to share . . ."

Sharing a personal story, while not pertaining to your brand much just yet (although notice the possible brand word *determined* that I threw in there), is a great way to start an open-ended conversation that will more than likely open the other person up to offering information about themselves as well. From there, integrate your elevator-pitch points and brand into the conversation, and you've got a great connection and a new member in your network.

A Story

A blogger reached out to me once for an interview with the CEO of the company I worked for. She was a mom and made sure I knew it by telling me how she was keeping her kids out of the heat and how they were out of school and making her work life more chaotic than usual; all fun, anecdotal stories that told me a lot about her personal life and career. Not only did she get an interview with my boss quickly (I enjoyed talking to her, so I wanted to help her out), but she also mentioned in her conversation with me that she marketed apps. That set off a whole new business relationship because our company was launching an app. If she had simply approached me wanting to talk to my boss and hadn't told me stories about herself, we would have never made that great connection.

Travel

Remember a few chapters ago when we talked about traveling, both domestically and internationally? Use every one of these trips and experiences to your advantage by growing your network in other parts of the state, region, country, or world. While traveling you will learn about new cultures and see different places. This can be the perfect opportunity to broaden your professional horizons. This includes simply traveling around your own country—or even your own state.

I challenge you: Get in the car, and drive somewhere different to meet new people and see what they deem important about your industry. This can mean setting up an informational interview with someone who has your dream job, but in a different area than where you live or plan to live. Don't just call or conference with them; drive over and meet them face-to-face. Don't get me wrong—I am a huge believer in technology and how it can help and serve us, but meeting face-to-face in an area you aren't used to can open your eyes much more than a simple phone call or Internet video chat ever could.

While traveling you will probably also notice different personalities in different areas, or even in different companies. The type of people you enjoy working with may also impact the type of place you choose to work. If you prefer the fast-paced multitaskers, you'll know that you crave that type of work environment, and vice versa.

A Story

In college traveling was an eye-opening and career-making moment for me. I went to a conference on the other side of the country with college students from across the nation. All of them were as motivated and excited as I was, they all had their eyes on similar jobs, and many were better equipped and prepared than I was to join the job market. Did this scare me? Yes. I was a big fish in a little pond where I had come from. This realization was tough, but I managed to use it to motivate myself, and that conference was the reason my peers and I started the student-run PR firm, got involved in new social networks, and increased our network. Our new friends from that conference helped us start the firm and were a great resource for us as we continued to grow ourselves in preparation for our careers.

How to Network

I don't know about you, but when I first heard about networking I imagined a huge hall filled with a lot of business-minded people wearing name tags, carrying around business cards, and trading pens and other giveaways with business logos on them. But what I've learned most about networking over time is that it definitely doesn't end (or even begin) with shaking hands and trading business cards.

Growing your network takes a fun and personable attitude and the brand you've created. You need to show people why they should want to know you and the vast amount of knowledge you've accrued by immersing yourself in your niche, but networking also requires so much more of you. It takes nurturing. Just like you can't call your mom once a year and expect her to be happy about it, you can't connect people in your network just once in a blue moon, only when you need advice or help. You have to make yourself an invaluable asset and an important cog in their needs wheel as well.

Let's take it step by step.

Introduce Yourself

This is where your branding, elevator pitch, and conversational know-how kick in. We've shown you how to brag about yourself and have them eat out of your hand. Never sell yourself short, and remember that you are worth their time and are important enough for them to want to make that first connection. Then make a great first impression, and you'll have them coming back for more.

Always give people you network with some material to remember you by. Most of you will probably decide to hand out a business card, but if you are at a career fair or event that would allow you to be a little more out-of-the-box, get creative! Either way, make sure everything you hand out is clean, easy to read, and professional. My favorite rules are as easy to remember as 1, 2, 3: Only use *one* graphic or logo, *two* typefaces, and no more than *three* contact lines.

One Graphic or Logo

If you don't get an automatic business card from your job, don't be afraid to create your own. This is actually very fun, and I recommend highly overusing a boring professional card. You can make your card vertical, use different types of paper or foil instead of ink, experiment with different-shaped cards (think square or round), and on and on. If you have a logo, use it. If not, make your name or initials interesting, or even make a design out of them. What is important here is to not do so much that you confuse the eye; rather, make your business card creative and different so that it stands out from the rest.

> Tip: At the very least, make a simple business card on a site like VistaPrint.com or OvernightPrints.com. They make it easy, and their prices are really reasonable. These are the two sites that we have used successfully, but there are lots that are similar out there— so shop around.

Two Type Faces

Never use more than two typefaces, or fonts, in one document or on a creative piece. Using more than two can not only confuse the eye but also make your card look messy or difficult to read. This is the rule with invitations, business cards, reports, or anything you would show anyone. It can be tempting to use more fonts, and you might even think it would look good. Don't do it! And another good rule is to try to use sans serif fonts for headers and serif fonts for body copy (i.e., all the other words). Serif fonts are so called because the letters each have a "serif" detail that finishes the stroke. Examples of serif fonts are Bookman, Cambria, Garamond, Georgia, and Times New Roman. Sans serif fonts are those without the small projecting "serif." Examples are Arial, Calibri, Century

Gothic, and Tahoma. It is pretty widely accepted that the sans serif fonts are easier to read in large bodies of text, so attempt to use those in your nonheadline copy.

Three Contact Lines

Try to limit the ways you want people to contact you to three. I know in this age of technology you probably have a cell phone, e-mail, Facebook account, Twitter handle, LinkedIn profile, Instagram account, Pinterest boards, and Tumblr you want them to follow, or maybe even a regular blog or a website. I beg you to narrow it down and decide what content is most important for people to know. This should be important in your organizational skills as well. The fewer ways you have professionals contacting you, the easier it will be for you to organize your correspondence and respond. I know it is tempting to put every network on that card to prove you know what you are doing online and have a huge network, but shy away from the twenty-line business card and share that information later. Not only is a simpler, cleaner presentation of your information easier for people to digest, but it will also save you the headache of checking every network every day for important business contacts.

For example, imagine you've given every network to everyone you see, and then imagine you've decided to not check your LinkedIn account or you're on a vacation from your computer for a long weekend. You could miss out on a great opportunity, or time-sensitive project, aside from looking like you are actually disconnected because you didn't respond in a timely manner. If you were to put your website, e-mail, and Twitter handle on your business card, you could set up e-mail alerts for when people contact or mention you on Twitter, link your website mail to your e-mail, and then only need to check your regular e-mail for important notifications from new contacts. And on your website (or in your e-mail signature) you can list all of your other networks. That's not to say that you should ever ignore your other networks, but you should simplify their management, which in turn will ease your mind a bit.

Listen

The most important part about having a conversation is listening. You have two ears and one mouth, and this ratio was created on purpose!

Use everything in its appropriate proportion. Listening will enable you to hear what the people in your network need, and then you can find a solution (or even a direction toward a solution) and grow the relationship.

Find a Connection

This goes beyond just a "Hello, how are you?" When you engage in a conversation with someone, try to find common ground with them. Did you grow up near where their aunt lives? If so, is it possible that you went to school with one of their cousins? Or maybe you and this person played the same position in the same sport growing up. Finding a shared point of interest can make you more memorable to them and make it much easier to continue the relationship later.

WIIFT (What's In It For Them)?

This is the most important question you should keep top-of-mind while having a conversation with anyone. Why should they have a relationship with you? Why should they put in the effort? Figuring this out early on can help you grow your network by proving you are an invaluable asset. Always offer advice or help when you can; this could even be as simple as sending a person in your network an article you think they would find interesting, as we discussed in chapter 5.

The main idea is to give first. Then give again. And then give more. Without asking for anything in return, give as much as you can. I can promise you that you will always get more out of your network than what you put into it. The more you can give, the more people will want to help you.

What could be helpful to you here is the concept of *reverse mentoring*—when less experienced, younger people mentor more experienced, older people. *Reverse* makes sense, right? We traditionally think of older-to-younger mentoring. As you are on the lookout for mentors—or an advisory board of sorts—to add to your network, the best thing you can do for many of these wise, "seasoned" people is mentor them where they might need it. You might be surprised to find that you know a lot more than they do in the area of technology (mobile or otherwise), social media, or cultural trends or that you are more familiar with an unconventional or modern way of doing things. This is where your knowledge can be used to your advantage.

A Story

I always looked up to my professor as a mentor, sounding board, and guide for any question I had in my career path. She always had a sensible answer but never gave it to me unless I asked for it and even then would refrain from answering if she thought I needed to make the decision myself. It was a great relationship, and for a long time, I tried and tried to give but never seemed to catch up. The first time she needed help with creating a website, I jumped at the chance to help her. I listened to what she needed, studied up on it a bit more to make sure I was doing the best I could for her, and then built it out. I made sure to ask for help from my network along the way. (Remember, you can always do things better when you have more heads than one.) When the project was finished, she was grateful for the website, I was happy to have another piece for my portfolio, and our relationship was that much stronger. Make sure to use every opportunity to help those in your network succeed. I promise that it will be a win-win scenario.

Brag

Notice that bragging comes *after* listening, finding a connection with the person, and finding how you can help them. And this is where the priority of bragging about yourself should stay. Once you've made that connection and the person knows your brand, you can show off a bit more and explain why you're a great asset to his or her company (or their friend's company). Go back to chapter 3 to remember how to brag the right way.

Make Sure They Remember You

Remember the phrase we used earlier, "It's not what you know, it's who you know"? Well, I dare you to take that phrase one step further: "It's not who you know, it's who knows you." Make sure to continuously nurture your relationships and reach out whenever possible. If you don't reach out, it's very possible that a vital member of your network could forget about you or that you won't be top-of-mind when they have a great job opportunity land on their desk or arrive in their inbox. Don't let that happen! Keep them updated with your progress, and send them (purposeful) e-mails from time to time.

Learn When to Say No

This is extremely important but also very difficult for a lot of people (including me). I know that while building your network and getting started on your career all you'll want to say is yes, but it is imperative to know when to say no. If you don't learn when to say it, you can get yourself in a lot of trouble. At best you will completely stress yourself out or lose sense of your priorities, and at worst you could forget or run out of time on an important project. And then you appear flaky, which is the biggest brand-killer of all time. Don't let that happen. Pay attention to your schedule, and keep a constant list of your priorities and what needs to get done in order for you to succeed. Always keep in mind that your brand is only as good as your worst day. Make sure you only commit to what you know you can do well and never more. Don't overpromise—only overdeliver. And how do you say no? Check back to chapter 7 to see how you can let anyone down easily, using our ready-made phrases.

Now you're ready to network: Take every opportunity to talk to anyone you can. Show them how you stand out by first listening, then helping, and always reach out as much as possible. The more work you put into your safety net(work), the more you'll get back; so start now!

Cheat Sheet

- Why network? To get a job!

- Who should you network with? Everyone.

- When should you network? Always.

- Use your student status.

- Take advantage of a limited-time audience.

- Where should you network?
  - Everywhere
  - Meetings
  - Travel

- How to network:
  - Introduce yourself.
    - Give beautiful material.

- Listen.
- Find a connection.
- WIIFT? What's in it for them?
- Brag.
- Make sure they remember you.
- Learn when to say no.

CHAPTER NINE
USE NEW MEDIA AND ONLINE TOOLS
Tori and Professor Hays

Are you out there in the social networking world? If not, you should be! It's how hiring managers are searching and finding out who you *really* are, as true transparency has become essential in all areas of business. Even if you just create social networking accounts for the sole purpose of getting a job, it will be worth it. You will learn more than you can imagine from these sharing networks and, we bet, it will be hard for you to stop engaging once you get your dream job. What's stopping you? Have you been afraid you'd get addicted? Or worried that you will "waste" time with these networks? Don't be. This chapter is going to cover everything from the basics to best practices, tips, and more.

New Media Crash Course

Even if you are a social media guru (which you should never say, by the way—but we'll go over that a little later), this section will be helpful because it's always good to review the basics and understand why you should put effort into each specific network as well as the best way to do so. We'll try to show you the importance of each, along with their differences and strengths, so that you have a clear understanding of what the best networks are for your available time and situation.

Facebook

Most people already have a Facebook account, and many times people are shocked if someone doesn't. If you don't, it's not the end of the world, but we highly recommend you set one up. Facebook is a great advertising tool for you and your brand. You can set up your own profile, add details about your education and employment, and post some pictures that make you look professional and hirable (we'll cover the don'ts later in this chapter). Facebook gives you the ability to share photos, video, links, original thoughts, and major life events (especially with the Facebook timeline).

The Basics

On Facebook you have a *wall/timeline* where you can post your own content, and then a *news feed* lists content from yourself, your friends, and your *likes* (usually causes, brands, or public figures). When someone posts content, you can then *like* their content (clicking a button that shows you like it), comment on it, or share it on your wall/timeline or a friend's wall/ timeline. This builds popularity for that content and gets it more noticed on the news feed (and makes people very, very happy). As just mentioned, you can also like causes, brands, and public figures whom you think are important to your own personal brand, or even like things you just think are fun and would enjoy having in your newsfeed. After liking them you will see their content populate your newsfeed, but you can always change the settings regarding how much you see and from whom.

After you are all set up, you can share some of your other accounts (including Twitter and Pinterest) on your wall/timeline using third-party apps. This can be a great way for you to share your content across multiple networks and garner more followers on different accounts.

Once you've got the hang of Facebook, probably one of the most important things to be aware of are the privacy settings. When setting up a Facebook account, or even if you've had one for years, be sure to check your privacy settings—often. Facebook is notorious for changing their settings without warning, and while you think you've got it all handled and private, sometimes everyone can see everything.

Best Practices for Facebook Privacy Settings

You should make yourself searchable, but that doesn't need to apply to every part of your life. Tori has her Facebook account set so that people can find her and see her education, employment, bio, and general details but nothing else. This lets her easily control the snapshot that employers get, and then she gets a warning if they want to be her friend in case anything needs to be cleaned up or updated. This is also just good practice in not oversharing. Another way to protect yourself is to set up an approval system for when you are tagged in anything. We would especially recommend this to people who (1) work in social media and need constant control of what is going out about themselves, (2) have friends who don't understand or don't care about professionalism, or (3) want to have control of which pictures of themselves are plastered all over their profile. This feature has saved Tori more than once from having unflattering pictures or posts that she didn't want plastered on her wall/timeline. It's also great for when you are on vacation and not monitoring what people are posting. The feature saves all the posts, pictures, and places you were tagged in on a list for you to review and approve when you are ready. It's like a Facebook privacy assistant!

Facebook Fan Pages

While we wouldn't recommend you set up a fan page for yourself (at least, not yet), it is important to understand the usability in case you ever do need to set one up. Once you have an account on Facebook you can set up a fan page and then add any of your Facebook friends as administrators of the page. Then you can post content on that page to be sent to the news feeds of whoever is following. There are easy ways to share the page through your account by messaging friends or by sharing it on your wall/timeline or on friends' walls/timelines. You can advertise each post or the page in general using Facebook ads or sponsored stories. It is pretty inexpensive and can get the page a lot more likes in a quick amount of time. You can also integrate other networks in fan pages the same way we mentioned with your main wall. This is highly recommended for larger brands because some people may not want to hear about you on Facebook, but if they see you have a Twitter account, for example, they might decide they would like seeing your content come to their devices that way.

Tip about Consistency: Many of you will have more than one social network, and you may even end up with a Web page as well. Make sure that everything with your name on it represents your brand and that it all has a consistent look (colors, graphics, profile pictures, etc.). You want people who engage with you on different networks to always feel like they are engaging with you and not with you and your thirty-eight different personalities. This is a basic graphic-design concept, but it is also a basic brand concept as well. All of your stuff should look like you. And all of it should look consistent.

Twitter

Twitter confuses a lot of people. And we'll admit it—it confused us at first, too. What is really great about Twitter is that people can decide what they want to use it for and then tailor the experience to fit what they want. Tori, for example, uses it as a way to receive news, share interesting articles, get her sports team updates, follow generally funny people, and keep up with her sister and friends. Professor Hays uses it for branding herself as an expert in the areas of public relations, collegiate success, entrepreneurship, and happiness. She also bonds with other San Francisco Giants and 49er fans via Twitter posts as well as the occasional post about her four-legged best friend and eighty-pound lap dog, Max.

Twitter is a microblogging tool that was originally text message–based, hence the reason for its 140-character post limit. Best bet is to join Twitter online (www.Twitter.com) and then get text notifications from Twitter on your cell phone from users you specifically select. Let's repeat that in case you missed it: *You can specifically, carefully, and selectively choose certain people you follow on Twitter to receive updates from on your phone.* Twitter is blamed for being an oversharing network where you receive too many notifications about things you don't care about. Trust us, it's not the network that is the problem in these cases—it's the user. Take the time to learn how to use Twitter properly, and this won't be a problem. It can also be a great tool to keep in-the-know for those who are less technically sound or who don't want to invest in a smart phone—it can all be done via your computer and text! Everything can also be done through your smart phone and a Twitter app. It's entirely up to you.

Twitter Basics

When you set up a free Twitter account you select a *handle*, or username (this looks like *@yourname*). Try to pick something shorter and easy to type (hopefully your name, but we'll talk about that a little later), so it's easier for people to share things you post, or to mention you in their own posts. Then you can include a short bio and a picture. We recommend a close, well-lit picture of your face for this network because the image is very small on most browsers. You'll also want to pick some *followers*, meaning people whose posts will show up on your Twitter page. You can follow whomever you would like by clicking on *follow* online or clicking on the appropriate button on an app. The more people you follow, the more content you'll get, so you want to make sure you manage this accordingly. Most users follow more people than they can keep up with and just accept that they will miss things. This is the sane way to use Twitter, which Professor Hays equates to drinking from a fire hose. She loves it, but she knows she'll never be caught up on Twitter.

Then go have some fun! Start *tweeting* (updating), and be sure to give people credit for their content by putting their username in your posts. This is called *at replying* or *mentioning*, because when you *tag* someone on Twitter, it looks like this:

@BetsyHays Thought of you when I read this [link].

You can set up your account so all of your @ replies come to you via text message or smart-phone app through a notification. If you really like something someone tweets, *retweet* it by either clicking the *RT* button online or in an app or copying and pasting their content and putting *RT @theirname* at the beginning of their post. Or you can put the message, and then something like "via @ToriRTerhune" at the end of your tweet. It's all about giving recognition to those who created the content. Watch a few people interact with Twitter and you'll get the hang of it pretty quickly. You can also *direct message* or *DM* users, which is a private message, meaning only they can see it. You can do this either by selecting the button online or in an app, or by typing *DM@theirname* and then your message. These direct messages are also restricted to the 140-character limit. Direct messaging is a great way to get in touch with someone quickly when you don't have their cell-phone number (provided that he or she is an active Twitter user). Also, you can only DM someone who is following you and whom you are also following. You may @ reply to anyone you would like.

Start following people who have similar interests, who are in the same field, or whom you just find plain interesting. Watch how they interact with Twitter, learn what you like and don't like, and tailor your Twitter experience the way you prefer. Quick tip on privacy with Twitter and gaining followers: We don't recommend setting up a private account on this network. When you are private people can't see your tweets at all. It makes it difficult for people to follow you and blocks your network from going as much as it could. If you are worried about spammers, there are verification services that could still be annoying to potential followers, but at least they can see why they would want to follow you in the first place.

If you are uncomfortable with the public nature of Twitter, don't use your city or your employer or other identifying information. Also, don't tweet about going places; only tweet about them after you have gone and returned.

If you're having problems finding people on Twitter, try using lists. Twitter lists are created by users and are generally based on specific interests or types of people. You can go in and follow someone's list to group-follow a lot of people. You can also search based on your interests to find people who tweet a lot about things you like.

Once you've gotten the hang of Twitter, you'll undoubtedly notice hashtags and want to use them. Hashtags started on Twitter as a way to see trending topics—for example, *#NewYearsEve*. They have become much more than that now, as they are a way to easily search, watch trends, or spread Internet memes around the Web. You can start experimenting with hashtags by simply finding words in your posts that you think people would search and putting a # in front of the term. For instance, you might want to tweet "I'm reading a #book on how to get a #job before #graduation by @torirterhune and @betsyhays—www.LandYourDreamCareer.com."

Once you start tweeting more, you'll most likely notice that you don't like the URL links taking up most of your posts. Try using URL shorteners. Most applications for Twitter have URL shorteners built in, but a quick online search will find you plenty of free tools to use. This will allow you more space to write your content around the link you are sharing. Professor Hays likes www.bit.ly to shorten URLs, and Tori uses her third-party scheduling application that has a shortener built in.

Twitter also has a personalization feature to it. You can personalize the background of your feed with colors, images, or—if you're really bold—additional pictures and information in a specially designed layout that shows to the left of your feed. If you are a designer, look up the dimensions and have fun! If not, don't worry; there are plenty of free services and templates out there to help you design something you'll love. We recommend putting other places people can connect with you in your background, like a website or a reference to finding you on Facebook or other network, as well as showing some of your personality. This will make you stand out to those recruiters and hiring managers.

Both of us love Twitter for a lot of reasons:

1. It makes people get their point across quickly (you only have 140 characters to do so).

2. It is easy to follow posts from specific people or brands on your phone or other mobile device, whether you have a smartphone or not.

3. Sharing links (to articles, photos, video, etc.) is easy and quick using either Twitter or third-party applications.

4. It is a wonderful way to receive news and be at the forefront of what is going on in the world—giving you a lot of conversation starters and just making you a more interesting person in general.

5. It is easy to have multiple accounts for different purposes, but we don't recommend this for everyone. If you are online every day and want to share with different audiences, you can set up different accounts to do so. For example, Tori has both professional and personal Twitter accounts and uses them completely differently to reach different audiences and keep from annoying her non-social-nerd friends or her professional connections. Again, we don't recommend this for everyone, but it is an op-

tion, and it works for her. (IMPORTANT TIP: If you have two accounts on any network, don't use your name on both. Tori's personal account is harder to find to reduce confusion.)

6. It is easy to integrate Twitter into your other social networks easily by repurposing the content, favoriting tweets to share later, and putting your Twitter feed on other pages (i.e., autofeeding into LinkedIn, and so on, so you only have to post once but people who follow you on different networks can see the content; we'll cover more on this later).

A Story

In preparation for a national conference, Reganie, a PR student at Fresno State, started a note on the Facebook group that had been created for the conference so that everyone could put their Twitter handle in it and follow or virtually meet people before the conference even began. It was great in theory, but because of Twitter's follow quota (which limits the number of people you can follow at a time to limit spammers on Twitter) it was hard to follow everyone without committing to coming back to the list hours later (after the quota limit had been lifted) and putting in a lot of effort to add people piece by piece.

Since she planned on following everyone anyway, Reganie decided to make a Twitter list, and then she shared it on the event's Facebook page so people could follow the list as a group without maxing out the quota Twitter allows. She also spread the word on Twitter using the conference's hashtag for people who hadn't connected on Facebook. It was successful on multiple levels: The list was shared by national committee members, other conference attendees, and others, and she became known as "the girl who made the Twitter list"—which spread her name around, grew her network, and grew her brand as a knowledgeable and tech-savvy student.

Reganie enjoyed making that Twitter list so much that she did the same thing before the next conference. That time she knew the influence it would have and grew her network immensely with little effort. Since then, the conference lists have remained popular and are requested again from new members. It was a win-win situation, because she made new connections and friends and it saved others attending the conference a lot of time.

The above is a great example of not only mastering the use of social media but also being innovative and creating a space where you can be successful. Reganie shared free information and put in some extra effort and in the end received much more than she gave.

LinkedIn

LinkedIn is one of the most important networks you can have when job searching. It is possibly (along with Facebook) the first place hiring managers will search for you to see information to supplement your résumé and application. LinkedIn allows you to list your bio, education, employment, interests, and strengths. People can also endorse you or write recommendations for you, right on your profile. You also have the ability to update your status so people can see what's new with you and your work, or you can keep them updated with articles that you find interesting or important to your field. I've never seen anyone use LinkedIn incorrectly, but we'll go over the basics, just in case.

Back to the Basics

Setting up a LinkedIn account is so easy because the site literally walks you through setting up an account, step by step. They have a percentage system that shows you how close you are to completing everything you need to do to have a full account, from entering your bio to adding connections and filling in each position you've held. Then LinkedIn will recommend people for you to follow based on where you went to school, where you've worked, and your contacts. Connect with anyone you want in your professional network, and then get busy engaging. LinkedIn is also a great place for you to search and find people that have your dream job in any area and set up informational interviews.

Photo Sharing: Instagram, Picasa, Flickr, Etc.

Photo sharing is all the rage, and there are several sites and applications that are specific to just that alone—sharing your favorite photos on the go. While these sites and applications aren't tailored to job searching, necessarily, you can link these accounts into your other accounts to make it easier to edit photos and share on the go if this is something you like to do. Instagram, for example, allows you to upload photos and share just through that site or also via Facebook, Twitter, or other sites. You can easily edit and share photos with your choice of networks at the tap of a finger. This can be a good and bad thing, so make sure that when the smartphones are out you are acting within your brand, and you won't feel bad later.

Blogs: Blogspot, Wordpress, Tumblr, Etc.

Blogging is an excellent way to show your interests, thoughtfulness, and writing skills. You don't necessarily have to write about your industry, although I'd recommend it, but you should definitely write about something that interests you. Not only will this be good for the job search and showcase you as an original thinker, and maybe even a thought leader, but it will also be really good for your own personal development and help you organize your own thoughts.

Think about blogging as public journaling. You jot down your thoughts and feelings about a certain topic, and you can get as personal as you want, but make sure it's brand building, because people *will* be able to see it. Then share your passions and cover all the topics you want to talk about. You'll surprise yourself with all your opinions, and your written-communication skills will soar—which is a great asset in our online world.

YouTube

YouTube is a great tool for sharing content and showing why you are awesome. You can share industry-related videos, learn how to do pretty much anything (including how to tie a tie), and show off your interests to your network. You can either create your own videos (pretty easy if you have a webcam or smartphone) or share videos of others in your network or of the geniuses of your industry. Think of YouTube like a video blog—or vlog—to share your thoughts with the world. We'll discuss how you can use YouTube to your advantage in your job search in chapter 11.

Pinterest

Pinterest started as an online pin board for people to visually share what they love, whether it be crafts, style and fashion, home renovations, wedding planning, decorations, or anything else visual. It turned into a great way for small online shop owners (like those on Etsy) to sell their wares and go viral. A few tech-industry companies have also used it to share articles with images showcasing the content (i.e., tech tools to travel with, etc.). We recommend at least checking it out and understanding it so that you can decide if it's a good way for you to keep in touch with certain aspects of your industry.

Instant Messaging: Skype, AIM, Google Chat, Etc.

Instant messaging, or IM, can be a great resource both personally and professionally, especially if you work remotely or are working with a group on a project and want your communication documented so you know you are all on the same page. Most services will allow you to create a chat room where you can create a water cooler–type interface for your whole team to check in quickly and ask questions of one another. You can also use IM one-on-one to quickly get in contact with someone when you can see they are online. This will usually get you a very fast response, as long as it is the appropriate way to communicate with that person.

If you want to use IM with people but don't want random people to message you, with most services you can change settings so only certain people can see when you are online, or make yourself invisible to anyone else online so that you can see when the person you need to talk to is online and then reach out to them. IMing may seem a bit more intrusive, but it is definitely effective when used properly.

Skype is another wonderful way to connect in a more personal way, as it allows parties to talk face-to-face, always the most effective form of communication. You can see people's expressions and nonverbal cues that really enrich any conversation. Skype, like all of the tools mentioned above, is free and is also a fun way to meet or talk with people in different cities, states, and countries. More for fun than necessity, Professor Hays Skypes in alumni guest speakers to her classes from different parts of the country each semester. The students love it, and the person being Skyped in gets to feel like a celebrity. All good!

MySpace

This is an older network, and not necessarily the most important for job searching, but it is still a good network for certain circumstances. MySpace is especially great for music-based or -related industries. Bands and record labels love MySpace; it continues to be a resource for finding new music, and it is a worthwhile place to express yourself through HTML personalization of your profile.

Back to the Basics

Similar to Facebook, on MySpace you have a *profile* where you share all your own content, and then a *feed* where you can see content from friends and those you follow. You can share photos, videos, content, and links; join groups; and friend pages as much as you want, as well as personalize your profile using HTML (there are also free services and applications to help you figure this out).

You'll notice that MySpace and Facebook are very similar services, just with different audiences, so you simply need to decide if people you want to connect and share with are on this platform as well.

Personal Website

Create a personal website. Do it, and do it now. This is the single best thing you can do for your brand, and it's not as hard as you might think. Even if you create a simple, one-page site as an online business card, you will be amazed by what it does to your search-engine optimization (being able to be found when people search for you online) and general networking.

First, before you do anything else, buy your name URL—*www.your name.com*. If it's taken, decide what other name you want to use for your brand and buy it. Seriously, do it now. Put down the book and buy it. It is usually around $10 per year to keep and is a wonderful investment in your brand and future. Then, if you aren't a computer programmer, or don't have a friend or dorm mate who is one, take to the Internet and locate one of the many free services that you can use to design your own site. Google Sites and WordPress are what we generally recommend. Both are free and pretty user friendly. Many URL hosts offer free website development and then charge a small hosting fee—a great, inexpensive option.

Once you start building it, make sure the look and feel of your site is consistent with your personality and the feel of your brand. Put your bio up, which networks they can find you with your username, what makes you different, and—if you're really good at this—your résumé, pieces or examples of your work, a contact form, feeds from your other networks, and more. The sky is really the limit here.

Online Portfolio

As part of your blog or personal website, it is a great idea to include an online portfolio. This means you show samples of your work and why people should hire you. Whether it's images, PDF documents of your written work, or links to other sites where things you've done live, having one place online where hiring managers can find anything you've done makes it much easier on them, and you, for that matter. When you're applying for jobs and internships and people ask for samples of things you've done, rather than having to find things on your computer or online and e-mail them individually, you can just send the link to your online portfolio. Trust us, not only will they be happy that everything is easy to find, they'll likely love your professionalism and notice how organized, prepared, and skilled you are. If nothing else, it's definitely a way to stand out from the crowd.

There are online-portfolio platforms (free and fee-based) that you can use, or you can use a source like WordPress and build it from there. Professor Hays's students all create an online portfolio in their writing class, and the campaigns class is now doing them as well. While this has a different slant than your personal online portfolio would have, here is a pretty good model using WordPress: YosemiteCampaign.WordPress .com.

How Not to Get Overwhelmed

Is your head spinning? We wouldn't blame you. There are many other industry-specific social sites out there beyond the many we've detailed already here, which you should research. If it is important to your industry, get involved. Keep in mind that you don't need to be active on *every* network out there, but you do need to keep your brand updated on the important ones. Creating accounts on all these networks seems like a daunting task. The good news is that is there are tools out there to help you. Once you decide how you want to use each of these networks, decide where some overlap can happen.

NOTE FROM TORI: I like to use Facebook, Instagram, and Pinterest for personal use, LinkedIn for professional use, and two Twitter accounts—one personal and one professional. To keep all these networks under control, I use integration built in to the applications and sites, combined with a third-party app, Hootsuite, which lets me schedule posts and manage most of the platforms. From this third-party application I schedule professional tweets, LinkedIn, and Facebook posts. From my phone I can share Instagram photos through Facebook and my personal Twitter with the click of a button, and Pinterest stands alone as a hobby-feeding and window-shopping experience. From this, you can see that I have one central place for my professional updates, one for personal, and one for my "fun time" online.

NOTE FROM PROFESSOR HAYS: I primarily use Facebook and Twitter, and I do it the old-fashioned way without scheduling posts. When I boot up my computer, several windows open: my e-mail, Facebook, Twitter, Pandora (for background music), and an online stopwatch (remember chapter 7). I spend a few minutes coming up to speed with recent Facebook and Twitter posts, and then I get started working. As inspiration hits for posts or tweets, I post or tweet, aiming for one to two Facebook posts and five to ten tweets per day. I also use Instagram on my phone, and usually I take and post one picture per day. As for LinkedIn, my tweets are linked, so they post there as well, so I only open LinkedIn when I get a message or request to connect with someone. I also don't feel obligated to engage in the evenings or weekends unless I want to. It's all very manageable with a plan!

Location, Location, Location

Another thing to consider is which social media sites are popular in your geographic area. Regions and states adopt things at different times, and what is popular in Oregon might not be widely used in Alabama. Find out what is important both where you go to school and where you intend to work postgraduation.

New Media Tools

Another way to handle all your networks at once is through tools and third-party applications. They can help you schedule posts and manage your accounts and the amount of notifications you receive. A few of these include Hootsuite (Tori's favorite with wide usability), SocialOomph (scheduling posts), CoTweet (managing multiple Twitter accounts), Compete (statistics and data on your pages or websites), Klout (measuring your online influence), Monitter (real-time Twitter monitoring), and Tweetdeck (Twitter management). There are several others out there, but this is a shortlist to get you started on the path to easily managing your accounts. Find out which tools make sense for you, and then research and learn how to use them to their full extent. It will take more time upfront but will save you *so much* time later.

When you experiment with your networks and different applications, you'll learn which networks and applications you prefer to update from, what's best for you, how to keep the clutter down, and (as we said in chapter 7) to always remember to breathe.

New Rules for New Media Communication

Now that you have added new or social media to your communication channels, you have many, many more ways to communicate with people. But which is the best way to contact those in your network? The first rule is to simply ask people which form of communication they prefer. Everyone will happily tell you. This is your primary guideline as far as the best channel to use, but keep in mind the following as well: Many conversations can be less painful, and much shorter, when the right channel is used.

E-mail is best for:

- *Information that is not urgent.* We generally recommend responding to an e-mail within twenty-four hours, but if you need an answer right away, twenty-four hours may not cut it.

- *Circling back on conversations and meetings.* Either notes or confirming who will do what by when.

- *Reminders for upcoming meetings or events.* This can also be done by calendar applications, but many people e-mail reminders anyway.

TIP: Create a signature in your e-mails that helps people know who you are and how to contact you. That can be your favorite network or the one you check most often. It can also include your phone number (if you answer it) and your best internship or title at the moment, whether on or off campus. To reduce confusion, keep it to a few line items, just as you would on your business card (check back to chapter 8 for tips on this).

Phone calls are best for:

- *Things that are urgent.* If you need to know something within an hour or if a deadline is pending.

- *When you are angry.* Even messages from the most gifted writers can come across the wrong way. If you are angry or upset, just take the time to call so your inflections can be heard. We also recommend taking several deep breathes and counting to ten first.

- *Things that are complicated.* Written communication can make this worse. When you can tell that this issue will lead to fifty back-and-forth e-mails, save everyone some time and pick up the phone.

- *When someone calls you.* Try to respond back to the person who reached out to you the same way. They showed you their preference in the first step, so rather than e-mailing to follow up a phone call, pick up the phone!

In-person communication is best for:

- *When you need to correct behavior.* If you need to let someone know they messed up, face-to-face is best. This way you can show your nonverbal messaging as well (whether it is anger or sympathy or empathy) and can also accurately gauge the reaction, as well as clear up any miscommunication.

- *When you need to acknowledge that you messed up and apologize.* Which can be common as an intern while you learn the tricks of the trade.

- *When you need a favor.* It's always best to use proper body language (lean forward and put your hand over your heart) and a great big smile when you need something.

- *When you are really angry or upset.* Taking the time to think it out and then using body language and seeing the person can usually be best in these situations.

- *When you haven't seen the person in a very long time.* It's always good to make sure you keep connected with those you don't see often enough. Even video calls are great for this purpose.

- *When you are interviewing someone.* Informational interviews or job interviews are usually best in person because you can make your best impression.

Texting is best for:

- *People who like texting.* You will quickly learn those who text you back and those who will call to return texts or are slow to answer or engage via text. Read between the lines and be intuitive.

- *When your information is time-sensitive but uncomplicated.* If you need to blast a quick time change to a contact about your meeting or a reminder about something coming up.

- *When the answer is short and easy to give.* A quick question with a yes or no answer, or if you need to remember the time for your meeting later in the day, or even a quick check-in to say hi to a friendly contact.

- *Now that most phones can text pictures, this is also a great use of texting.* Texting a picture to share an idea with a contact, or something beautiful or funny or powerful, can really go a long way. Pictures with words are the best ways to communicate.

Social media is best for:

- *People who prefer social media communication.* If you know your connection is always on Facebook but takes forever to respond to an e-mail, try Facebook. Same with Twitter—if you notice that they are tweeting away, DM or @ reply them in a tweet asking your question or sending them the reminder. As with all social media, keep public tweeting positive (i.e., don't tweet that someone is late to a meeting or missed a deadline).

- *When having a conversation in a public forum is appropriate or helpful.* If you are starting a thoughtful discussion or found an article, video, or post that you think they will find helpful, share it on their network. Not only will they appreciate the thoughtfulness, it will also make it easy for them to share, grow the conversation, and increase your network.

Instant messaging is best for:

- *People who tell you they want to use it.* Some people *hate* it and find it weirdly intrusive (Professor Hays is one of these), but some people love it (Tori is one of these and a frequent user both personally and professionally).

Own Your Own Name

Pull out your computer right now and search your own name in quotes: "Firstname Lastname." Put the book down and search it. Did you see anything about yourself? Did you find out you have an extremely popular name? If you have a common name and there are a lot of results, consider adding your middle initial to your brand or using a nickname. Try searching that. Keep trying until you find a name that makes you unique but that you also enjoy and feel fits you and your brand. It may be tough to go a little different from what you're used to, but we promise it will be worth it later when you are the top search result and distinguishable from all those who have the same name.

You might be second-guessing us here, especially now that we're asking you to front some cash and change your brand name. So why is search-engine optimization important? And why should you buy your name URL? Here's the deal: Hiring managers *will* search your name online. They like to see what's out there, and if they can catch you doing something that goes against your brand, you could be toast. Similarly, if you are hard to find, it will be difficult for you to stand out. A great offense is your best bet here. If you buy your URL now, believe it or not, www.yourname.com does much more for searchability than www.Facebook.com/yourname. One reason is because your actual name is in the URL. Search engines love that. You can also fill the site with keywords that you find important to your brand. When describing yourself in your bio and creating the meta-tag description (the one or two sentences that show under the site title on the search-engine results), make sure to repeat those brand-centric terms you decided upon. This will drive your message home. Then you have complete control over all content on the site. You can post whatever you want and keep it updated to showcase the best version of you.

Now that you've bought your URL, start searching all the social networks and reserve your name on all of them. That's right, all of them. When someone searches for you online, you want to be easy to find, recognizable, and consistent. The last thing you want to do is confuse someone who could potentially hire you. Even if you don't intend to use them, sitting on the username will keep anyone else from grabbing it and potentially messing up your brand.

A quick example: If you get your name on everything but Twitter, because you've decided you don't like Twitter, someone else could grab that name easily. Either intentionally or unintentionally, they could start posting personal stuff about themselves: how they went drinking in Vegas, how they love to show up at work late, how they hate their boss, and so forth. And pretty soon their Twitter feed starts showing up in search results. Then when hiring managers search your name and that Twitter feed pops up as the second or third result, they will see it. Even if it's not you, don't assume that the hiring manager will take the time from their busy schedule to triple check their facts. It will harm your name and brand. So get your name now while it's available and, if nothing else, put your bio and picture on it, a few interesting tweets, and leave it. At least it will be really you and true to your brand.

Best Practices

Frequency

So how often do you post? Generally this will depend on the network that you are using. Our opinion is to imagine you are following someone; how much *valuable* information would you want to have them give you on a given day? Think about this on each of your networks, and decide on a formula. Your formula should start with X amount of posts per day, X days per week. On Facebook, for example, we recommend at most two per day, whereas on Twitter you could go up to ten per day (spread out a little, and a lower number like three to five is fine). You can do this without oversharing to those different types of followers. Here's a general rule of thumb to help you out:

microblogging/quick image sharing where people only really care about the content being posted that second:

Twitter/Instagram/Pinterest = 1 to 10 posts per day

profile-based networks where people are interested in your profile and connections as well as posts:

Facebook/LinkedIn/MySpace =
1 to 4 posts per day, not necessarily every day

longer content-related networks where people expect more in-depth, thought-provoking content, as well as longer responses; give yourself the time to do this right:

Blogs and YouTube = 1 to 3 posts per week

The next part of your formula is the content. Always be mindful of what your audience wants. They want information, and they want you to be yourself. If all you do is repost content that other people post, why wouldn't they just follow those people? Here's the general rule of thumb: Always strive for at least 60 percent value-added content, with the remaining 40 percent about you and your personality and brand. Of that maximum of 40 percent content about yourself, only 5 percent should be promoting yourself. No one likes someone who brags all the time, so make sure you keep it interesting, and only talk about yourself when it's really important, or if someone else says it and you repost, retweet, or share it. (That's the best kind of self-promotion because you didn't even have to say it!)

So this would be a weekly example formula for Twitter:

3 posts per day $\times$ (.6) 60% value
content $\times$ 7 days = 13 value content posts to schedule

3 posts per day $\times$ (.4) 40% me
content $\times$ 7 days = 8 me posts per week to schedule

Not a numbers person? Don't worry. Just keep in mind that you always want to post more value-added items than not. Strive to only talk about yourself one out of every three posts, at the most, and that is a great start.

These formulas are incredibly useful, especially as you are learning these networks, but also as you continue to grow your influence in the social world. These can be great guides as you search for information to share and as you check to make sure you aren't oversharing your own life and can help you determine when you are done posting or scheduling for the day. Formulas also release the pressure of the perfect post. You know that you are always posting good, consistent content to your followers, so you can be less worried about getting it perfect every time.

Going Viral

Everyone wants to go viral; you want your content to be viewed a lot and enjoyed, otherwise why would you post it? The question is how to get that edge to take your video, post, or image viral. In general, most often it's content that people can use and want to share that goes viral.

The Litmus Test for Posting

When it comes to Facebook and a few other networks, we always get push-back from students who demand that they have their private life on Facebook but still want it to be kept private. If this is your current thinking, we have some bad news for you: Your online life is *not* private. No matter what your privacy settings are, or even if you delete certain posts, never assume anything is private that you post online. One person can take a screenshot of that post before it's deleted, and the next thing you know it could be everywhere. Also, people can hack accounts and see whatever they want on your account without your having any idea. There are tons of stories out there about how people have been fired for posts about their bosses or workplaces that they were sure were private but got out anyway. We'll say it clearly for you: *Your life online is not private.*

You may think that social media is about connecting with your friends and sharing everything that you have inside your brain with them, but the truth is that social networking sites provide brand-building or brand-killing opportunities. It's really that simple, and if you fight this truth, you'll be very disappointed, and probably unsuccessful.

This is where true transparency comes into play. If you decide to have a life online, be smart and know that people will see it. Then, please, make smart life choices. Everyone loves to go out and have a good time, but you definitely don't want that picture of you upside down doing beer bongs and Jell-O shots getting circulated to your potential boss. Have a rule with your friends that you don't take the camera out drinking. Or, if you take a camera, make sure that the pictures stay in the camera and don't appear online. These are the times when mental pictures are best anyway. Take a nice picture of everyone before you go out, as this is when you'll look your very best. Enjoy the moment you're in, and leave the cameras and phones at home or in your pocket.

Go on the offense via social media. Start adding posts, pictures, and content that help build your brand. For example, pictures of you volunteering or taking a trip abroad are great ways to show your well-rounded personality and worldview. If you have a hobby that you love (beside anything illegal—just a disclaimer), your networks are a terrific way to showcase it. Don't think that snowboarding will turn an employer off of you; it might actually do the opposite. Employers want motivated, interesting people to work with. Plus, you never know, your next boss could have the same interest as you do!

A Story from Tori

I was looking to hire someone, and I had a slew of applicants. Many were recent graduates, and it was hard to make a decision. As I started taking phone interviews, the applicants were all starting to run together and becoming hard to remember. Then, on one phone call, an applicant expressed her interest in gymnastics. I was coaching cheerleading, and we had a great conversation about the sport and working with kids. Then we realized that we both also had an interest in working with the deaf. Needless to say, I recommended that applicant and she was hired. Was this applicant qualified for the job? Yes. Was she the best person for the job? Possibly. Did she get an edge from sharing her hobbies and interests? Yes. The lesson: Share that you are an interesting person, and managers will appreciate it.

Here are some quick questions to ask yourself before ever posting anything online:

1. "Do I want Grandma to see it? What about Mom? What about my next boyfriend's or girlfriend's mom?"

2. "Would I want it on the front page of the newspaper?"

3. "Does this post help build my brand?"

> TIP: If the answer to any of these questions is no, don't post. If you're not sure, don't post. A great general rule is that if it doesn't build your brand, it doesn't belong in your public world.

To make it even easier, below are some quick do's and don'ts for posting online.

Do:

- Create suitable profiles.
  - This means using an appropriate picture, adding a readable and interesting bio, and filling it with your background so people know who you are. This is the first step in being successful in social media.
  - Make sure your profiles are also consistent so managers and recruiters know when they have found you.
- Use social media for public praise.
  - Shout-outs, kudos, and anything positive about others are always welcome and appreciated. People love to "me too" and like and repost these types of updates. You'll probably be surprised how much attention you get by giving someone else attention. People love to say thank you and give you praise back.

A Story from Professor Hays

One of my former students sent me an e-mail a while back saying that it was National Mentors Day and that she wanted to thank me for helping her with her career. I was very touched and also got to thinking about my own mentors. Over the years I've lost all of their phone numbers and some of their e-mails but knew I was friends with them all on Facebook. So I wrote a post tagging my five amazing mentors. Imagine my surprise when I checked Facebook a little later, as I had about a dozen comments to my post—some from my mentors saying thank you, but many from people that I had mentored giving me praise. This was not at all the intent of

173

the post—I do public shout-outs on a regular basis—but the unexpected and lovely nature of what happened was very profound and a great lesson: Freely praise others and you, also, will receive praise.

- Be responsive.
  - ○ Don't ignore comments, mentions, messages, or anything where someone is trying to reach out to you. Not only will it hurt their feelings, but you could also come across looking uninterested in your network, and others will take note.
  - ○ On Twitter, if someone @ replies or mentions you, reply back. If they DM you, DM them back. If you get mentioned in a Facebook post, like or comment on the post. Always either like or comment when people write on your Facebook wall/timeline. When people send you a message, respond to it.
  - ○ Not responding online is the same as staring at a person without responding when they are talking to you in person. It's rude and will not move you toward the accomplishment of any of your goals.
  - ○ A twenty-four-hour turnaround for responses is probably just fine, but sooner is always better.

- Act like you do in person.
  - ○ One way to always do the right thing online is to think about what you would do in a similar situation in person. If someone asks you a question, you respond. If you are given a compliment, you say thank you. It's the same online, only more people see your good or bad manners!

- Give lots of useful information.
  - ○ People love free knowledge; they eat it up. The human mind loves to learn new things and always wants to be the first to know everything. The more interesting and breaking news you can give your followers, the better. You'll become a resource for people in your network, and that is invaluable. The other great thing is that once you give out enough free information, people may be willing to pay you to get more—or maybe you could even write a book!

- Say thank you.
  - Say it, and say it often, for anything anyone does. It makes you look appreciative in public and get some notice even though you're giving someone else praise.

- Be authentic, genuine, and transparent.
  - Just as we discussed earlier, your online profiles and accounts should be the best version of your true self. Be true to your brand, be proactive, and keep it clean so you don't ever have to make excuses in a job interview.

- Listen and engage.
  - Listen 70 percent of the time, and respond the remaining 30 percent. You have two ears and one mouth, so keep that in mind when you are online. People do love to learn new things, but they also like to be recognized, so make sure you do so. If you really listen to your network, you can respond with relevant information and be much more valuable to your followers, besides making them feel good because they know you are paying attention.
  - This also means actively liking and commenting (authentically) on Facebook, commenting and retweeting on Twitter, and commenting and liking on Instagram and Pinterest. Show others that you are engaged with their content, and they will be more likely to engage with yours.
  - However, be selective with your likes and comments, and make them count. If you like everything, it's the same as liking nothing. And if you comment on everything, your comments cease to have value.

Don't:

- Don't be negative.
  - Ever. Remember what your mom (hopefully) always told you: If you don't have something nice to say, don't say anything at all. Treat others the way you would want to be treated, and be kind in general. This is always better for

your brand and your general disposition, and you'll make more friends. We promise.

- Don't post when you're crabby or angry.
  - If you are mad or in a bad mood or having a bad day or are sick, don't share it online. Many people do this, as you know, but you have probably also observed that this doesn't build people's brands. It makes people think that these people have issues or are unlucky or just have a miserable life. Not what you want them thinking of you.
  - If you really need to talk about what's going on, text your best friend or call a family member. These are the few people who really need to know about all of your trials and tribulations. The rest of us don't.

- Don't respond when you are crabby or angry.
  - If someone did something to hurt you, you're stressed out, or just plain are in a bad mood, don't respond to anything if you think you can't be nice. Take up to twenty-four hours to calm down, breathe, and really think about how you want to respond, if at all. Remember that what you post online stays there forever, it can always be taken the worst way possible, and others will read it. Take your time. It can wait.

- Don't cause drama.
  - Save the drama for your mama! Seriously, keep the drama off the Web. Passive-aggressive posts about people in your network when you're angry or calling people out online is a bad idea, always.
  - If you are unhappy with someone, call them or see them in person. Those are the only two choices you have.

- Don't ever assume you are a social media expert.
  - Or a guru. For two reasons: (1) you can't be (it hasn't been around long enough) and (2) it can make you (honestly) look like a jerk. Be humble and appreciative. Know that you can always learn more and that no one really has mastered social media. Social networks are all about learning from

one other, so take advantage of this rather than assuming you are the end-all, be-all.

- Don't be a bull in a china shop.
  - Don't run in and jump all over things as soon as they are posted. Be polite, patient, and quiet at first, and then share your voice. Then you can really form your opinion and respond in a thoughtful, value-added post. Being the fastest isn't always the best.

- Don't be inappropriate.
  - Keep your brand in mind here, and watch what you say. Keep your language in check, and watch any sexual references. Making people feel uncomfortable, even if you're joking, is never a good idea when you want to be on their good side. Remember that the written word can always be taken the wrong way and that everyone can see it, so be careful what you post and really think before posting.

Cheat Sheet

- New media crash course: understand your networks and how to use them.
  - Facebook, Twitter, LinkedIn, photo sharing, blogs, IM, MySpace, websites, online portfolios

- Don't get overwhelmed.
  - Select your networks carefully.
  - Remember—location, location, location.
  - Use tools.

- New rules: know how to communicate with others.

- Own your own name and brand.

- Know best practices.
  - Frequency and formulas
  - Virality
  - Litmus test of posting: Don't post if it won't build your brand

- The do's and don'ts of social media:
  - Be responsive.
  - Act like you do in person.
  - Give lots of useful information.
  - Say thank you.
  - Be authentic, genuine, and transparent.
  - Listen and engage.
  - Don't be negative.
  - Don't post when you're crabby or angry.
  - Don't respond when you are crabby or angry.
  - Don't cause drama.
  - Don't ever assume you are a social media expert.
  - Don't be a bull in a china shop.
  - Don't be inappropriate.

BECOME AN EXPERT
Tori

N ow, if you were paying attention in chapter 9, you know that we told you to never call yourself an expert—when it comes to new and social media anyway. But that doesn't mean you can't *be* one! Both in your networks and in your field, you should always strive to be perceived as an expert at what you do. It will be obvious to employers and your connections that you are ahead of your peers and fellow students, and that is how you get hired.

Find Your Niche

Every industry has certain niches for professionals. If you are looking at going into a broad industry, like engineering, marketing, communication, teaching, nursing, or business, start thinking about what you would like to hone in on, and then focus your efforts to make yourself stand out.

For example, if you are studying business, you can take extra courses in international business and foreign languages and then study abroad to back up your interest, get more real-life experience, and, of course, enjoy yourself and make sure you like that side of business before you graduate. If you are studying engineering, consider getting a minor in something completely different, like biology or music.

Take advantage of the plethora of information around you while you are a student, and add courses to your schedule that will supplement your primary major and get more than what all your peers are getting. Remember, the more you have over them, the better off you are. It's not always a competition—and you shouldn't pit yourself against your peers who will help you much more than hurt you—but you definitely don't want to be in last place when you need to compete!

While it is a great idea to try to be well-rounded, most employers want to hire someone who is really good at something specific. If you're good at everything, but not great at anything, they might go with that other applicant who is less good at some things but amazing at something valuable for the position. The best way to get hired is to become an expert in a certain aspect or niche of your industry. You will need to find a piece of your industry that you are passionate about and become extremely involved in that area.

A Story

I wasn't always passionate about social media (now my favorite part of my career). I grew up in a conservative family that didn't even have Internet access at home. I had to go to school, the library, or my friends' houses if I wanted to do research for class, send e-mails, or check MySpace (back before the days of Facebook). I think this actually helped me a lot, though, because when I got to college I was astounded by the amount of information I could attain online whenever I wanted. I fell in love with communicating online. Then, during my senior year of college, I learned about Twitter and the amount of collaboration that could take place on one network alone. That was when I decided social media was my niche. I was passionate about it, and I really thought I could make a difference for people in this field. It was a growing industry, so it was easy to make a mark. I learned as much as I could, testing my own accounts, creating accounts for other people, and experimenting as much as possible on my own time. My efforts were noticed by my network, and before I even graduated I had spoken to three different college classes on entrepreneurship, social media, and job searching; had earned a rookie award for my overall industry; was being called upon by local businesses for my opinions; and—most importantly—held a career-related job!

A Story from Professor Hays

When I was in college, part of me always thought that I should get my teaching credential in addition to my public relations degree. I ultimately decided against it, opting to graduate sooner to begin my "real life." I was fortunate to get a job with an amazing public relations firm not too long after graduation and spent two years building up my career and moving up the ranks at the agency. I loved public relations, but I couldn't shake this nagging feeling that I wasn't quite in the perfect job. Then I moved to Arizona and, obviously, started there unemployed.

Not being able to get rid of the thought that maybe I should try teaching, I signed up to be a substitute teacher. I subbed a grand total of three times, and, for lack of a better way to describe it, the children ate me alive. I was terrible, and I didn't even have a clue how to be not terrible. It was very upsetting, as I clearly wasn't meant for that career path. So I went back to public relations, and one day, while I was giving a seminar about something that I can't even recall, I had my aha moment. It wasn't teaching that was wrong for me—it was the age of the students! I was made to teach adults, not children. And, because I really did love my industry, it made sense that I was made to teach public relations. Given this understanding of myself, I started on my master's degree and have been happy in my niche for the fourteen years since its completion.

Once you are on the right path, you'll know it, as you won't let anything stop you. I remember carrying my first daughter up the stairs to my professor's office when she was two weeks old so I could turn in a paper. I took my mom with me for logistics and moral support, and neither of us thought anything about the incident was strange. You do what you have to do and you make it work when it's the right thing for you.

Get Passionate

Another great reason to focus in on a specific area of your field is that you can get really passionate about that one area and, if necessary, reenergize yourself on your career path. I know that when I first got involved in social media I had a brand new appreciation for the communication field and could see how much this new area was going to impact my industry. This niche got me really excited, and I now had a different view of what I was going to do in my career and how I was going to make my mark on the world. This passion made me feel ready to tackle anything my senior year, which is when most college students will tell you they are most nervous about what the world holds for them. And that passion extended beyond just me. Others could see my passion and got excited with me, wanting to either learn from me or hire me. Get passionate about what you are doing, and the rewards will flood in! Plus you'll be happier, too.

Be Authentic

Coupled with being passionate is the importance of being authentic. You are you, with all of the unique and wonderful gifts that entails. Embrace these gifts, and work with them instead of against them. If you are funny, artistic, or witty, go with it! Also, go with *all* of it, for while we can and should always strive for self-improvement, essentially we are who we are and need to be the best that we can be using what we have.

A Story from Professor Hays

I am quite loud (as in voice volume), and all my life people have made comments about it. It used to really bother me, and I would try to not be so loud. Well, somewhere along the line I decided that being loud was authentic to who I am and I should try to embrace it rather than attempt to change it (which didn't ever work anyway). So now I joke with my students about maybe not sitting in the front row for their own safety. I use my gifts of projection when I do public speaking, and often I don't have to use an annoying microphone. No one has ever asked me to speak up, so I know my voice is always heard.

Bottom line: Be who you are. If people don't like it, you can all move on. The world is *full* of people, including lots who will love pretty much everything about the authentic you!

Use the Internet

Whether it's searching how to do something, watching YouTube seminars or free webinars to broaden your horizons, or utilizing your social-network discussions (like LinkedIn groups, Twitter live chats, or Google Hangouts), you can learn so much for free from the Internet. It's far easier than buying more textbooks and much more fun than going to more classes. Strapped for cash and can't afford the laptop or smartphone? Try your local library or school computer lab, where they generally let you use the computers for free.

Save Yourself Time and Energy

Focusing on a niche within your industry will also save you time, as you'll be focusing your efforts rather than trying to be great at everything. We offer a lot of juicy information and tips in this book, but if you try to use every bit of everything in every aspect of your industry, you won't have given yourself any wiggle room. Plus you'll give yourself a headache. Get the most from your time by focusing in on a piece of the industry that you love, and you won't have to worry about knowing everything about everything. Just know everything about one or two things, and you'll be set.

But You're Still a Student! So What?

Now you might be asking yourself (or this book—metaphorically, of course!) how it's possible to be an expert when you aren't even in your field 100 percent of the time yet. Trust me, it is possible, because I've done it and I've seen others do it too. Just because you are young doesn't mean that you aren't smart. You can learn a lot by implementing what is in this book, through informational interviews, internships, conferences, and more. Through these experiences (sometimes even more than in class, actually) you will learn important lessons by doing, which is what is incredibly valuable and looks great on a résumé. But the really wonderful thing is that no employer really expects you to truly be an expert. They know you are a student, and they will simply love the effort that you put into becoming a major player in the field. Your enthusiasm and motivation will show the potential employer that you have the self-starter attitude it takes to be great at your job. That's right. Being an expert (or showing true efforts to become one) can lead to your dream career!

How to Be an Expert

This heading sounds great, doesn't it? "How to be an expert." I wish there truly were a formula for how to become an expert at anything, but there isn't. I have yet to find a surefire, foolproof way to become an expert (and if you do find the expert formula, please let me know). But I can promise it will take a lot of work. A lot of it is simply applying nuggets from other chapters in this book to your specific niche. You'll see how applying pieces of these steps to your industry niche could make you the best at what you do—or at least make others think you are. The steps and tips below will definitely get you on the right track toward having others in your field keep you at the front of their mind.

Find a New Niche

If possible, try to find a niche that is in an up-and-coming part of your industry. Something brand new and shiny will lend itself to newcomers who are able to learn as much as (or even more than) the people who have been in your industry for years. It will also show that you are on the cutting edge of your field because you are already involved in, and maybe even leading, the thoughts and opinions in that area.

> NOTE: That's not to say that you can't choose to focus on the professional area you really love just because it's been around longer; you may just have to work harder, research more, and be louder to get noticed.

Speak About Your Niche

While you're a student you are offered an incredible array of clubs, groups, and classes always eager for new information. Shop yourself and your niche around to those who might be interested. Don't ask for anything in return (yet), because what you are getting is invaluable material for your résumé and portfolio. You are showing the world that you know enough about your niche that others will sit and listen to you. This is *huge* for those just starting out. Plus it's always good to work on your public speaking skills; you don't know who could be in the audience. (Refer back to chapter 2 for tips!) Perhaps you are speaking to someone who could become a connection for the job you've always wanted. Or you could find a new, similarly minded friend to bat ideas back and forth with.

Showcase Your Talents and Knowledge

Get Awarded

We covered this in chapter 3 by telling you to get involved outside the classroom, but trying to get awarded for your specific niche is even better. There's no better way to tell people you are great than having other people say it for you, and if you have an actual plaque or trophy stating that you are the best, even better. These awards could be from professional associations, on-campus clubs, or any group related to your industry, professional- or student-oriented. Try to get more than just academic awards, though, because while both are good, employers won't spend much time looking at your GPA.

So apply for everything you have time to apply for, and enter as many contests and competitions as you can.

Become a Thought Leader

We touched on this in chapter 9; you can create a blog to share your thoughts about your industry and create original content. Use your networks to expand your reach, research a lot to learn as much as possible, and then get creative in your posts. For example, before I was writing this book I was writing a blog around public relations, marketing, and job searching. There are a lot of student blogs out there on these subjects, so I tried to get creative in my posts. I talked about my favorite brands and what they were doing and what I thought some brands could do better, and then I threw in some information about myself and the influence I was having in my department when it came to social media (without bragging). This last post was one of the main reasons my first boss after college wanted to hire me; he agreed with my ideology in the industry and even e-mailed my blog to his network because he wanted to share his thoughts as well. So start getting creative and start writing. Start with a blog, and maybe one day you'll be writing a book!

TIP: Even if you're not a great writer and don't feel like this is applicable to you, try to push through it. Do short, two-paragraph posts; talk about articles you found and whether you agree with them or not; find infographics related to your industry that you think people will find interesting. (Hint: If *you* think it's interesting, others will, too!) Post interesting images or video that relate to your industry, along with a quick bit of text to make it personal to your blog. It doesn't have to be much, but it does have to be *something*. As we discussed in chapter 2, written communication can do a lot for your professional brand because it always makes you look smarter and more committed, as you are the one putting in the extra effort.

Make *Expert* an Unspoken Part of Your Brand

The key here is to never, ever call yourself an expert. Just strive to be one at all times. People will decide for themselves how much they value you and your opinion, so make yourself valuable to them, and be original and transparent. If you can't think of the answer, search for it. If you get back to that person before they figure it out, it won't matter where you got the information from—you will have been the source to that contact, and they won't forget it.

A Story

I had no idea how to do anything you're learning about in this book when I started college (not so long ago). I was organized when it came to classes and planning my schedule, but it was more out of a fear that I would never graduate and would disappoint my parents than out of an effort to be proactive. So I met with people smarter than I was, learned what I needed to do, and stayed on top of it. Later, when I started my first business, I had no idea what I was doing then, either. I started searching online about how to start one and then used resources on my college campus to learn the rest and get support. When it came to job searching and how to interview—I'm sure you've noticed the pattern—I had no idea how to do that either. The point is that I picked each piece up slowly, learned how to do it from my network or on my own, and then shared my journey with others so they could learn from my mistakes.

Cheat Sheet

- Find your niche.

- Get passionate.

- Be authentic.

- Save yourself time and energy.

- But you're still a student! So what?

- How to become an expert:
  - Find a new niche.
  - Speak about your niche.
  - Get awarded.
  - Become a thought leader.
  - Make *expert* an unspoken part of your brand.

CHAPTER ELEVEN
PUT IT ALL TOGETHER!
Tori and Professor Hays

Now that you've learned the ten steps you should be taking in college to land your dream career, it's time to take everything we've talked about and refocus it even further toward your job search. Think of this as grad school for the content in this book. Are you ready to take it to the next level? We thought so. Just by reading this far you've proven that you recognize the importance of standing out (in a good way) and how these nonacademic items will make the difference between a so-so career and a dream career. So take a moment to feel good about yourself, and then read on.

As graduation approaches, you can use what you learned in each chapter to ramp up your job search efforts by expanding on what you have been doing.

Step I: Start Now

Just like we encouraged you to meet with your professors and advisors early and make connections, it's never too early to start making connections with human resource (HR) people and those in charge of hiring decisions. As you know, being a student is a very strong tool in the job market. It's not necessarily about asking for an actual job interview but perhaps just sending an e-mail to the HR person expressing interest in the company and also doing many, many informational interviews.

And just like we encouraged you to craft a solid plan toward graduation, you should also create a target list of businesses you might want to work for and start reaching out to them now. Create a plan for where you would like to be when you graduate, and start working backward to find the steps you will need to take to get there, as well as when to take them. This is very similar to planning out your courses over your college career—you need to know prerequisites and when your department wants you to take specific courses. (For example, some courses are only open to seniors or during specific semesters or quarters.) Real life is a lot like that, only without the written rules or roadmaps. Now is the time to create your own!

If you want to be in an entry-level position with an architecture firm by the time you graduate, then you need to make sure you know what that firm's hiring policies are. Do they tend to hire up from interns they've had previously? Do they use a third-party recruitment firm that favors certain internships or companies to hire from? This is all invaluable information that you can get pretty easily from an informational interview with someone who works there. How did they get hired? Do they know the hiring policies, or is there someone you can speak to that would? Then you need to make sure your coursework is set so that you have time to do your best work at the internships that will lead you to that job. Make sure you take necessary classes as soon as possible, and start interning right away to get on the right track. If you can even get an internship at that firm after your sophomore year, imagine how much they'll want to hire you by the time you graduate. You'll know their company so well and be able to jump right in.

Remember to collect business cards everywhere you go, even as a freshman. Talk to people who seem to really love their jobs, and jot down the names of those employers for future reference. Through traveling and the other tips in this book, you should always be on the lookout for jobs, companies, and environments that you would enjoy. When you find them, make sure you start networking immediately! It's never too early. Imagine the joy of a recruiter who has known you for two, three, or four years when she finally gets to interview you for a job—the comfort level and support will be amazing!

> TIP: Make notes to yourself on the back of business cards after meeting people. This way you don't have to rely on your memory. For example, you could jot down where you met them, what you talked about, any information you offered to get to them, and so on. This way you have all of the raw material for your follow-up conversation—whether that is in person or online.

Step 2: Design, Build, and Protect Your Brand

By now you should be in good shape in the area of brand building if you have used the tips in this book. In fact, now might be a good time to do a brand checkup to confirm that your brand words are still viable and that you don't want to alter them to make them stronger to fit your new, awesome soon-to-land-your-dream-career persona.

Take a moment to think about your brand words and how they apply to your job hunt. If you picked *positive*, are you being positive about your search? Make sure that whenever you speak to people you are upbeat and happy at the opportunity of finding your career. If you picked *proactive*, are you being proactive in your hunt? Be sure you are seeing what needs to be done before it's asked of you and doing it. If you picked *innovative*, are you creatively approaching your search? Find new ways of doing things, and make your mark by proving to others how you are innovative in *everything* you do, not just your job hunt. Just like you've been doing since you read chapter 2, keep your brand words close to your heart and your brain at all times. We know that job searching can be discouraging at times, but this is the perfect chance to use your actions to prove your brand to others.

Then you can work on becoming even more vigilant in regard to protecting your brand. Every office you hold in a club or organization, every volunteer opportunity you take on (whether it is short- or long-term), and all the jobs and internships you choose to take will all reflect on your brand. Choose wisely, and remember that you need to *be* your brand, not talk about how much you exemplify your brand. Actions speak volumes, and, unfortunately, bad actions speak the loudest.

Avoiding brand killers now needs to become your specialty; pay special attention to banning lateness, flakiness, poor writing, and lack of initiative from your life *forever*!

Remember your litmus test for everything, including social media posts. Ask yourself, "Does this help to build my brand?" If it does, do it. If it is neutral, don't do it. And certainly don't do it if it will definitely *not* build your brand or will harm it. This makes things a little more black and white, which is helpful in our world of infinite choices and many, many shades of gray.

Remember while on the job search to always dress appropriately, develop solid writing skills, be articulate, grow your vocabulary, be four-ish minutes early to everything, be ridiculous about gratitude and circling back with managers and recruiters, close communication loops, post and speak carefully and strategically, strive for HIC (honesty, integrity, and credibility), and customize yourself to your brand. If you want to refresh yourself on any of these points, turn back to chapter 2, because these are *all* important and basic steps toward protecting and maintaining your brand. And don't forget about your public speaking skills. Always remember your Ws and H when walking in an interview (who, what, where, when, why, and how). Continue to polish your presentation skills, even when you are simply presenting yourself during a conversation or an interview, and practice whenever you can. The better you can present yourself in front of others, the more others will want to have you on their team.

And here's your sigh of relief: Remember that you don't have to be perfect. No one is perfect, and we promise everyone else applying for that job you want has their issues, too. In chapter 2 we told you that consistency is more important than perfection, and that will be true forever. You just need to be what the company is looking for and stand out from the rest, and having a well-built and maintained brand is one of the best ways to do that.

Step 3: Immerse Yourself

Immerse yourself in your job search; eat, drink, and breathe it. Work on it at least a little bit almost every day, and be prepared for any opportunities that arise. As you get closer to graduation, your search needs to shift from a last-priority detail to a first-priority job. Give your job search so many hours per week, even early on, making sure that you stay on top of it at all times. Chase down the hot leads first—those most likely to get you closer to your dream career. The best way to keep on top of things is to not hesitate. When you get a lead for a new job, follow up on it right away. Often almost-grads will pause out of nervousness or anxiety, and those pauses can cost them their dream jobs. Immersion does not include pausing.

Many students graduate unemployed and then begin their job search, usually with some level of panic and desperation (often very destructive twin emotions). If you are immersed along the way, you significantly increase your chances of being employed upon graduation. No need for panic or desperation. You've got this because you've been working on it all along.

Now is when you take advantage of the strong relationships you've created with your advisor and professors. Most times they will have connections off campus, too. Don't forget to maximize your involvement in university-affiliated programs; it's time for you to cash in on all the work you put into the clubs and associations you've joined to help your brand and job search. Most student organizations are affiliated with a professional association. This is the perfect opportunity to get the word out through connections and let the world know you need a job.

Remember that you still need to read, even if there isn't a recommended reading list. You've taken a great first step by picking up this book! And you don't have to read each book cover to cover; nonfiction books are not stories that have a beginning, middle, and climactic finish. Look through what you think is pertinent to you and your needs at the time, and read those portions. Then go back and reread as you see fit. Or not!

Be sure to take all those connections made through your internships, volunteering, and other involvements and put them to good use. Make sure you have letters of recommendation, and circle back with people in your network, past employers, internship supervisors, and coworkers to let them know you are looking for a job. You might even learn that one of your previous internship sites has a full-time position available and since you were such a fabulous intern they want to hire you right away.

Off campus, make sure you know recruiters and your potential hiring managers just as closely as you know your professors and advisors. If you've really been working at conducting informational interviews while a younger student (and even early on in your senior year), this will be an easy task for you. From your notes you will have an incredible amount of information about your higher-priority prospects and personal preferences and who and how they would like to hire. Your senior year is a great time to reach back out and let them know you're on the market. And that's when you brag. Always rehearse your bragging points before stepping into an interview. We discussed the best ways to do this in chapter 8, so go back and look if you need to. Interviewers love hearing stories much more than hearing your résumé read off to them. Use your responses—filled with anecdotes—to support your résumé.

Remember our tips about how to get an internship (as they work for getting a job as well): Use your network, be prepared at all times, brag, and use good manners. Once you land the job, remember to be a great employee for the company. After all, you may work for them now, but one day they'll be a reference on a résumé, and you want them to give you a glowing review.

Step 4: Employ the Magic of 75/25

Now you can perfect your use of the 75/25 rule by working toward *really* spending 75 percent of your time thinking and 25 percent of your time doing. Most people need to start by slowing down. If you spend way more time thinking than doing, then you will have to actually do less and what you do will be better. Look for places in your days and weeks where some scheduled thinking time can occur.

Think about your goals in your job search, prioritize them, and find out what needs to be done right now. Then, using the compounding effect, if you work in small amounts every day, you will get the best and biggest rewards. It's all about consistency here, and as long as you keep it up and make it a habit you can achieve more than you ever could trying to do it all in the last month of your senior year.

Carve out time to do all this thinking. Remember that a good time to ponder is while you are doing something else: walking, running, swimming, biking, driving, and so forth. (Don't get too far up in your head, however; you certainly don't want to hurt yourself by tripping or running into a car!) Others like to be singularly focused and just sit and think. Whatever works for you is what will work, so do it! Turn everything off, and then brainstorm your job search and ponder about what you could do better. Carving out time to do your life/time reviews will help you review your job search on a higher level. What is going well, and what isn't? Make notes on how next week or month could be better.

> TIP: Make sure you write down all of these thoughts. Have a job search notebook that you take with you everywhere. It can be small. Jot down all notes and random thoughts you have so they're all in one central place, and then use them as a guide during your review moments. Relying on your memory can be dangerous, especially when your potential career is on the line.

Think before you start anything. This is all about creating your roadmap, understanding all the steps you need to take, and working backward. Remember, your deadline is graduation day, and you have plenty to do before then!

Keep in mind that the more you think about your job search, the more creative you'll be. This is your creativity bonus. Rather than just sending a normal cover letter to a magazine (if you are a journalist), you may want to send them your own mini magazine all about you. One of Professor Hays's students inserted QR codes into the different parts of his résumé to send potential employers to his online portfolio. He also included the logos of the different companies he had worked for on his résumé to make it more graphically appealing. Another student made a project-portfolio CD to hand out with his résumé that had a label with all of the logos of the organizations he had worked with. This made the CD more visually appealing—and more impressive!

Always, always, always be accurate. Accuracy is much more important than speed in your job search. One misspelled word or broken sentence on your cover letter or résumé can ruin your chances with any manager or recruiter. Always be sure to check, double-check, and triple-check your correspondence and materials you send. If possible, try to have a friend, mentor, or parent available to edit for you. Remember, two heads are always better than one. Technical perfection is your goal with your application materials, as more than one person has lost a job opportunity by submitting a résumé filled with mistakes.

A Story from Professor Hays

During my initial job search after college, I was thrilled to have an interview with a firm up in Sacramento where I wanted to live.

I bought a new suit, made arrangements to stay at my aunt and uncle's house, and drove up for the interview. Imagine my surprise when it wasn't an interview. The business owner simply wanted to point out to me, face-to-face, that I had completely screwed up my cover letter. I had her name in the address line, but then I had "Dear [different name]." I wanted to cry, and I think I did when I got out to the car. In my quest for speed and getting out a lot of résumés and cover letters, I had sacrificed accuracy. And this woman had an opening, which added salt to the wound. But the opening certainly didn't go to me. I wish I could tell you that she and I are now friends and laugh about it, but I can't. Even though I lived in Sacramento for several years after this, we never really spoke again.

Kill your procrastination bug. Don't let the job search scare you so much that you put it off like the plague. Take control, establish limits, set up your physical spaces, prioritize, ask for help when needed, give yourself time frames and use timers, break work into smaller pieces, and understand the difference between acceptable and perfect. (Refer back to chapter 4 if you forget how to do any of this.) Trust us when we say that putting off the job search only makes it so much harder in the long run. Don't get caught along with your peers expecting an employer to come find you. That rarely, if ever, happens. Unless you are a star athlete, recruiters don't come to college students individually. But hard work and a plan will get you there; just take your (very) small steps to success one at a time.

One of the best ways you can also use the 75/25 rule in your job search is to be a problem solver. Employers love when an applicant can come in and solve a problem for them. Make sure you figure out before your interview *why* they need to hire you. Do they have a specific problem or missing piece in their business? Share how you can fix it. Come prepared with what you will do to fix things, and your name will stay at the top of their list. And remember, sharing this information early on before you even apply is better. Once you've made your connections through informational interviews, stay in contact and share when you see how you can help them solve something.

> TIP: Actually, this is more of a word of caution: Don't ever assume you know everything. This is the time to be humble and simply offer your two cents as an outsider. Always be polite and collaborative, never demeaning or a know-it-all.

We know you only have so much time in a day, so we want you to use that time wisely. Pay attention to your Priorities Right Now tasks, and at this point that includes everything that will get you your dream job!

Step 5: Master Every Conversation

Now all of your practice conversations are really going to start to pay off. The conversations you have in your job search will increase in importance, as it just takes one to lead to the interview that might change your life. So this is the time to polish the skills you learned in chapter 5 and step up your knowledge of your audience, no matter who it may be. Make sure you have specific goals for all of your encounters and that you circle back with yourself after each conversation to evaluate whether or not you reached your goals. If you didn't, try to figure out why. And then you can do better next time!

Make sure your elevator pitches include specifics about your job-search needs. Use conversation trees, giving the people you talk to at least two options to hang on to and further the conversation toward meeting your objectives.

With regard to adding something of value, this is where it gets even more fun. The value you add during interviews should really come in the form of free advice or resources. Share how you have a wealth of knowledge and can be a source of ideas for success for the business. Your circle-backs and thank you notes after interviews can include links and articles that relate to what you discussed during the meeting. Your goal is to make yourself indispensible, and the more you help their business, the more indispensible you become to them. Information is everywhere, so it's not hard to come by. The problem is that most don't have time to chase it down. This is where you can come in and provide resources that are useful to someone who doesn't have time to find it him- or herself.

Especially when you are prepping for an interview, don't forget to consume some news the day before and morning of the interview so you have plenty of conversation fuel. If during the chit-chat beginning phase your interviewer broaches a hot news topic, you had better have something to say. Depending on your industry, you lose the job simply because you were clueless about what's going on in the world. Employers want to know that you are plugged in, as this is how you can uncover things that might potentially help the business meet its goals. Many great ideas have been created from reading or listening or viewing a news story. Clients have been landed and partnerships have been created as well.

Bring your elevator pitches to your interviews. You know some of the questions you will be asked, such as "How are you?" and "What do you want to do after graduation" and "Why do you want this job?" Have great answers that showcase your brand and your ability to be the one they are looking for. When you are building your responses, remember to be the three Cs—clear, concise, and consistent. Particularly in a job interview, clarity is essential. This person is probably interviewing you at the expense of her other job duties, so her focus might not be laser-sharp. Don't be confusing! And the *concise* piece is crucial as well, as you want the interview to be a dialogue, not a monologue.

Remember to include some conversation trees in your responses as well so that the interviewer has a couple of directions to take the conversation depending on what interests them most. As you may recall, this is when you give two or three choices to the person you are talking to. For example, "My favorite parts of my major were the hands-on labs and the application of the discipline to current societal problems." This gives them two branches to metaphorically grab on to in order to continue the conversation in the direction you would like it to go.

The magic word *and* will also be your friend in a job interview, as it gives you the opportunity to always include what you want to say in every answer you give. In public relations we train people to bridge their responses to questions from the media to the talking points that they want to share, and the same rule applies here. Answer all questions, but before you finish talking add an *and* and then share something you want them to know. Other conjunctions may also be helpful, so don't forget about the magic word *or* and the magic word *but*.

Note that just like an elevator pitch is not supposed to be a monologue, an interview (oddly) is not all about you. It's a time for a conversation, with both you and the interviewer sharing information. The interviewer has a lot to tell you, and you will show a lot about your brand by the way you listen. The best interviews don't feel like interviews at all; they feel like you just had a nice time talking to someone interesting, and the interviewer feels the same way. *That* is when you get the job!

With any conversation, and a job interview certainly qualifies, remember to pay attention to your outcomes. Did you get the second interview or the job? If not, can you figure out why? Analyze what went well and what didn't, and use this information to improve for the next time.

NOTE: Always take the interview, even if you are not sure you want the job. Worst case, you get some interview practice. Best case, you get your dream job. *You can't lose!* (And how many situations in life are like that?)

Step 6: Innovate to Stand Out

Study how others are job searching. Ask your classmates and recent grads what they did that worked. Then do it better. Continuously question your strategies and tactics to verify you are on the right track. Make sure you are using your limited time wisely, and brainstorm ways to use that time creatively as well. For example, you could partner with some fellow students to create an internship fair for your major on campus. This gives you an opportunity to put another activity line on your résumé and also gives you great contact with everyone in your field that offers internships—networking and résumé building all at once!

Step up your traveling, and be sure about where you'd like to begin your career. Take advantage of holiday weekends, school breaks, or conferences and conventions to visit or revisit places you might be interested in. Schedule informational interviews with professionals in the places you visit to build your out-of-town network. It's usually easier to get a job near where you went to college, mostly because of your larger number of connections, but that shouldn't be a roadblock. Research the job markets, salaries, and standards of living in different cities to help you decide where you want to start your professional life. If you take the jump, you can still be successful, but you'll just have to work a little harder.

TIP: The longer you stay in one specific area, the more your roots will sink in, especially after you graduate and have to worry about paying the bills. If you know you want to move, or if you're even unsure, start taking the steps to get there. It is very easy to be complacent and get stuck in one area because moving is hard and finding a new job in a new area is harder. The great thing is, when you are a student, people are much more willing to help you find jobs in new areas; it makes sense to them that you would want to move after you graduate.

A Story from Tori

I knew I wanted to end up in the San Francisco Bay Area. Without any job leads or any idea of what I would be doing upon graduation, I put a nonrefundable $700 deposit down on an apartment while visiting during spring break. I considered it both a leap of faith and an investment in myself, trusting that I could figure it out as I went. I then found another student, a junior, who wanted to intern in the Bay Area for the summer and offered to share the apartment with her. At least, I figured, I had some help with the rent. Then, as I continued job searching, I implemented many of the things we discuss in this book, including searching LinkedIn and prodding people in my networks who knew others in the area. I ended up persuading the employer in Fresno who wanted to hire me to let me work virtually from the Bay Area and since then have received other jobs there. The idea is to trust yourself, make the big decisions, and don't be afraid. Be innovative, and you can make it work!

Step 7: Allow for Wiggle Room and Celebration

You might be feeling like wiggle room is a luxury you can't afford right now, but, ironically, now is when you need it more than ever. If you are flying through life in an overscheduled, semi-autopilot kind of way, you will miss things. You will miss opportunities and impromptu, spontaneous chances that often give our lives the most richness and meaning.

Take some additional steps *today* to give yourself a little more wiggle room. Shorten up some meetings. Don't overschedule yourself and, if needed, reschedule some appointments for a later date. Say no more often—and say yes to only what you need to do for your job search, what you absolutely want to do for your job search, and what you have time to do. Crush the one-more-thing habit. (Remember, that's the really bad habit most of us have that makes us leave late sometimes—or always.) Build time into your day to breathe, and get in the habit of getting up early, because most likely soon you won't be able to sleep in as often as you did in college. Be punctual to every meeting you have, and don't procrastinate.

This may be easier said than done, but make sure you celebrate this job search journey. Fortunately, for most people, their first "grown-up" job search is the hardest job search they'll ever have, so even that is worth celebrating. Beyond that, there will be happy milestones along the way. Don't forget to pause and celebrate them. Share your celebration with others, and they'll be excited for you too and want to help you more. Give kudos to all who help you in your job hunt liberally and frequently— send numerous thank you notes, and give those social media shout-outs! Schedule celebrations regularly, and also celebrate the specific milestones that you've set. For example, say you are really trying to get an interview with one specific company. Once you get that interview, even before you go to it, celebrate! Go out with your friends, and enjoy the fact that you've gotten one big step closer to your goal. Then celebrate again afterward, because we're sure you will be awesome (you *did* read this book!).

Embrace the fact that this is a very exciting time in your life—you are shaping your future! Enjoy every moment, and be thankful for where you are. As we've discussed, focusing on the good that is happening leads to more good things happening. Often life is about momentum, and you want to keep it flowing your way.

Step 8: Network, Network, Network

Now is when all that wonderful networking you've done over the past few years comes into play. Hopefully, through immersing yourself in your industry and all of your informational interviews you have a great network and really know the people you have been reaching out to and connecting with. So now we're going to take a different approach to the why, who, what, when, where, and how when applying networking to your job hunt.

- *Who*. Know who the manager or recruiter is. This should be an easy one because you can check back to your notes that you've kept from your informational interviews. Use as much as you can from those previous conversations. They'll be impressed that you remember everything and are more likely to help you out because you care about them personally.

- *What*. Research the company you are interviewing with. Read everything on the Internet, and talk to everyone you can who might know something helpful. It is amazing how many people don't even do a Google search prior to an interview. There will be an expectation that you know something about them. And the more you know about them, the more impressed they will be.

- *When*. Pick the right time to reach out to the company. That's why you ask this in your informational interviews. If a company hires for the summer in March, then you should reach out just before then to get any early information you can and get back in touch with that contact.

- *Where*. Remember when we talked about meeting people in person? This is especially important when you have a job interview. If you don't go in person, there are certain things that you will miss out on (including meeting others in the office and potentially growing your network and increasing your chances), and potential problems could arise (technology is not always our friend). So, if at all possible, make the trip and meet face-to-face. This is another great chance to pull on your network and find a place to stay with one of your contacts or friends.

- *Why.* Understand why you are connecting with the manager or recruiter. Know exactly what you want, whether it's an informational interview, a job, or a referral to another person at the company or in the industry, and so forth.

- *How.* You are a student, and employers love you for a few reasons. You are generally eager, excited, fresh-faced, and (while not always great for you) cheap. In fact, some companies would prefer to hire younger, less experienced individuals for those few reasons. Know that you can use all of this to your advantage, and be confident in your interviews.

Being involved in a network and helping others will now pay off. Remember to take advantage of your limited-time audience while you're still a student, and remember how much people in your industry love you right now. Help yourself by setting yourself up with beautiful personal business cards that stand out but are easy to understand. Listen to what your network members or potential employers need, and try to find a connection or how you could help them. Remember that the job hunt is really about *them*, not you. Try to anticipate their needs, and be proactive about meeting those needs.

Make sure you have strong letters of recommendation from influential members of your network, and only pick those top few. Having too many letters doesn't look good; it looks messy and can be potentially overwhelming. Any time you leave an internship or a job, make sure you get a letter of recommendation from your boss. *Always.* You never know how long your boss will be at that company or how busy they will be when you need that letter of recommendation by tomorrow. It's also tough for your boss, or connection from your network, to remember specific examples of why you were so great in your position if a lot of time has passed between your being there and your asking for the letter of recommendation. They'll remember that they loved you and you helped out a lot, but they might forget about that one presentation or project that was the turning point in your early career. Asking your boss or network connection to write a letter of recommendation is also a fantastic way to make sure they remember you. They'll have to put why they think you are wonderful down on paper and really think about it. This is great for you, as it solidifies all of that in their minds.

TIP: Never ask for a letter of recommendation from someone who hasn't seen your completed work up close. Most likely the letter will come across impersonal and may look like a template. Your letter of recommendation should always be personal to you and be specific about what you've done to be so great at your job and what you've done to impact the company or even your industry.

ANOTHER TIP: You might even want to offer some bullet points to the person writing your letter to help them accomplish the task, and sometimes he or she might even request this from you. You probably have the best ideas about what you'd like to have included, and they might appreciate your making their lives easier. We are all busy, and when others help us get things done relationships get stronger.

Step 9: Use New Media Tools

You now know all about many new media tools, and hopefully you have begun to use them the way they were intended—to help the world see the best version of *you*. Maintenance and monitoring becomes more important as you progress through your job search. Make sure the accounts you have chosen to have are active and that you are continuing to contribute good, valuable content on a regular basis. Remember the formulas we discussed in chapter 9. Create one for you, and stick to it the vast majority of the time. Consistency, quality content, and actual engagement (as opposed to one-way conversations) are the keys to new media and social networking success.

Responsiveness will become more important than ever, as many jobs are won or lost because of timely or untimely responses. Be sure you are actively monitoring any and all activity online and in your social networks; you never know who will give you the lead that gets you your dream job, so treat everyone that reaches out to you as if he or she were your next potential boss.

As you e-mail people asking for interviews, send them a link to your personal website or your best Web presence available. This makes it easier for the employer to learn more about you with little or no effort.

Set up a signature on your e-mail that links to your top three best-optimized pages or profiles. Try to keep it to three or fewer so as to not overwhelm. We recommend you direct to your personal website or blog and then to the top two networks you communicate through, because you'll be most proud of those and also communicate more quickly through them.

Create a video résumé, and share it on YouTube. There are plenty of fantastic examples of this online, and it can be a great tool to help you stand out. People love visual content, much more than reading, and you can use those bragging tips we taught you to supplement your résumé points and explain them conversationally. Make sure that you have a great background for your video (either interesting or a simple solid color—not white—behind you), that you look your best, and that you speak slowly and clearly. This video can be a generic offering about you and your strengths, and then you can tailor your résumé to each specific employer to be a little more customized to their needs. You can then e-mail the YouTube link to them and share it on your Facebook, Twitter, LinkedIn, and any other profiles you use to get your network sharing and watching your video.

Remember to only post things that build your brand or will get you a job. Otherwise, keep it offline and text it to your friends. Remember the do's and don'ts of social media, create original viral content, and rock the online world!

Step 10: Become an Expert

Just as chapter 10 trained you to become an expert in your industry, you should now become an expert in job searching. Sign up for job search newsletters, and read job-hunting blogs to get as much information as possible. Then find your niche *in* job hunting itself. Maybe you are really great at in-person interviews, writing résumés, or using social media to find new recruiters. Whatever it is, get really good at that one thing, and use it to your advantage in the job search.

And get passionate about that one thing. Show everyone how much you love to give interview tips, offer to help them with résumés, or help them set up their own social media accounts so they can find recruiters, too. Whatever it is, as you tell everyone and show your love for it, others will get excited, too. Remember, finding that one thing that you are really great at will save you *a lot* of time and energy. You simply don't have time to be excellent at everything at once.

Don't get discouraged thinking that you are just a student and that you won't be great at job searching. You are part of the market that is job searching, so you understand the hiring field better than anyone else out there. Use your free resources to learn more if you get stuck, and if you share the information you have with others, then people who are good at the things you struggle with will help you in those areas as thanks for your help. Really collaborate here, and understand that two heads are better than one, three are better than two, and your entire network is better than anything. Share your knowledge, and you'll be sure to get even more back!

If possible, try to get yourself out there on your campus, or in your area, to talk about job searching. If you've found that one thing and really understand it, speak about it. Offer to do workshops on résumé writing, interview skills, or new media and the job market. Believe us, people will *love* these topics. There are always people looking for jobs, and if you have valuable information, they'll want to hear it— especially when it comes from someone their own age.

You might even become a thought leader in job searching in your industry. In chapter 10 we discussed some really great ways to become a thought leader on a topic. Create a blog to write about your thoughts about job searching in your industry, and try to create original content. Use your networks to expand your reach, research in depth to learn as much as possible, and then get creative in your posts. Remember that there will be *a lot* of student blogs out there on this subject, so being creative and finding that niche will be key to your success. Even if you aren't a writer, remember that you can use examples, articles, infographics, images, and videos to share compelling content, and then add your original thoughts, opinions, and knowledge to it.

If you really do this right, people will be asking *you* for your opinion regarding job search tips in your field. And while being an expert in job searching may not be beneficial to your later career, focusing on your industry will certainly lead to more contacts, and this knowledge will always help you as you transition between careers. It will also help you stand out to job recruiters. Keep in mind, recruiters want to understand you, the market, your wants and needs, and where they can find people like you. That is their job. The more you can share with them about what you know (since you have researched so much and are a thought leader that people look to), the better you look and the more useful you are in their eyes.

A Story from Tori

In my senior year of college I set out to become an expert in social media and job searching. I constantly told and persuaded my peers that they needed to have a website, online portfolio, and well-built online network if they wanted to stand out at all in the job market. I got a lot of push-back from students who didn't feel that they needed to be online for their careers. And while either side could have been right (although I was one of only two in my department to have a job in my industry upon graduation), our arguments and discussion really helped me build my case and research more. It also made for great discussions on my personal blog, which, as I discussed in chapter 10, is why my boss wanted to hire me. And when I later was laid off, all of that job-hunting knowledge came in handy. I was on top of my game and less than thirty hours later had another job, better than the last.

Bonus Section: Résumé Tips

We encourage you to visit your campus career center for the latest information about résumés and cover letters. These centers typically have wonderful templates that you can use to customize your own materials. Once you have drafts of these items, bring them (in hard copy and in person) to your major advisor and ask him or her to review them with you. Please do not e-mail them to this person and ask for help. Show up in person so you prove you have some skin in the game, and sit down together to go over everything. The dialogue that ensues will be extremely helpful; busy professors and advisors tend to resent students e-mailing these things and asking for what ends up being a very time-consuming activity while the student isn't contributing their time to the task as well.

Make sure your résumé includes the following:

- A sentence about yourself (remember your brand key words here!) or what you specialize in. If you are applying for a technical job, make sure you list the programs that you are proficient in, as most companies will want to know.

- Your top few past positions and top contributions.

- The dates you worked at each position; if there are any holes, prepare yourself for interviewers to ask what you did in between. They'll want to know why you took time off and that you continued to work toward your goals.

- Related volunteer or organization work outside of your professional experience.

- Awards, scholarships, and other accolades.

- Your education, including any concentrations, minors, or certificates and your GPA. Only include your GPA, though, if it is outstanding. If yours isn't outstanding, leave it off—we doubt if anyone will ask for it—and if you are asked, tell the truth.

Résumé tips:

- Always be completely honest about your work.

- Do make it look nice. Browse free templates, see if you have a design-student friend who could help you out, or get creative on your own. Make your résumé clean and different looking. Think about what type of résumé you would want to look at if you were a hiring manager.

- Keep it to one page if you can. Then put supplemental info on your website, in your online portfolio, and on your networks. Pick your top jobs that you want to show off and the top few things from each of those positions. They don't need to know everything that you did, but they should see the best things.

Sometimes putting things in columns will help you get more on a one-page résumé.

- Do alter the résumé depending on whom you send it to. Because the résumé should really only be a page, you want to show off the most relevant and applicable work possible. Be thoughtful when you are applying, and find out what that company would want to see the most. Then concentrate on those few points.

- Don't include retail or random jobs (unless you have to). One of the best moments in your early career will be when you can have a full résumé without needing to use babysitting or sales associate positions. (Another time you should celebrate!) However, please do include them if you don't have much other work experience. Employers need to know that you've been a successful employee for someone else before applying to them. It is also important for them to know whether you put yourself through school, as this shows good time management and balancing skills.

- Give yourself credit. If you worked with a team to create something, don't leave it out just because you didn't do it on your own. It is still one of your accomplishments.

- Don't use the words *helped to* anywhere on your résumé. You don't help people do things—you do them! Make sure you give credit where credit is due, but you did it. Try using *collaborated* or something similar instead.

- Use verbs at the beginning of each line of your responsibilities under your professional and related work experience. *Managed, strategized, developed*, and *created* are some high-powered words.

- Use numbers—people love to see numbers on résumés. Did you help sales by X percent? Did you save the company $X? Did you manage X people? Did you lead a team of people or generate X leads or sales? Stick those numbers on there, and they will definitely stand out to the manager reading it. In fact, we've had a few managers say that they skim résumés for numbers to see how the applicant directly impacted their work. Numbers show true results and the return on investment for what a company was paying you. They can also pop out of the page and help you stand out from people who use only words—*25,000* stands out on a page much more than *twenty-five thousand* (and it takes up less room!)

Here is a sample résumé:

SUSIE KAY UNDERGRAD

123 1ST AVE. • SUNNY CITY, CA 12345
(555) 555-5555 • SUSIE UNDERGRAD@EMAIL.COM

SPECIALTIES

Media Relations	Social Networking	HTML Formatting
CMS Administration	Copy Editing/AP Style	Logo and Publication Design

SUMMARY OF QUALIFICATIONS

Account Supervisor   March 2012 – September 2012
Company 1, Inc.
- Managed interns and worked directly with clients to build and maintain a consistent brand across multiple social network platforms
- Increased click through rates in Facebook and MySpace ad campaigns by at least 200%

Marketing Coordinator   January 2011 – February 2012
Company 2, Inc.
- Strategized and implemented comprehensive PR plan and made presentations to the board of directors regarding PR activity and results
- Created an online archive of PR activity summaries saving organization $9,000 per year

Public Relations Intern   August 2010 – December 2010
Company 3, Inc.
- Collaborated in planning corporate picnic for more than 500 employees
- Served as PR consultant for 8 to 10 developing businesses at a time; including green tech companies

EDUCATION

California State University, Fresno   Graduating May 2014
Bachelor of Arts in mass communication and journalism – public relations emphasis
- Cumulative GPA 3.71

OTHER RELATED AFFILIATIONS/EXPERIENCE

- **Student Organization Treasurer and Webmaster**
- **Honor Society Member**
- **Freelance Journalist** for publications: A, B and C

HONORS

- Outstanding Public Relations Graduate, MCJ Department at Fresno State, 2009
- Rookie of the Year, Public Relations Society of America Central California Chapter, 2009
- The President's Volunteer Service Award, 2008
- Best Magazine Feature Writing from Fresno State Community Journalism Program, 2008

REFERENCES AVAILABLE BY REQUEST

Now What?

Now it's time for you to shine! You have more material in this book than you probably have time to use, and that is okay. Use as much as you can, customize it to make it your own, and make sure you take time to celebrate along the way.

We have a tremendous amount of faith in you and wish you the best in your journey toward your dream career, and we would love to hear how it is going. You can find us on Facebook on our fan page at Tori Randolph Terhune and Betsy A. Hays. We are on Twitter as well: @ToriRTerhune and @Betsy Hays. And visit our website at www.LandYourDreamCareer .com.

Best of luck!

INDEX

ABOUT THE AUTHORS

Tori Randolph Terhune is a 2009 graduate of California State University, Fresno, with a BA in mass communication and journalism with an emphasis in public relations. By the time she walked across the stage to get her diploma, Terhune had three years of experience in her field and an entry-level job in her desired industry. She was recognized as the Outstanding Public Relations Student by her department and as Rookie of the Year by the Public Relations Society of America's Central California Chapter.

As a student, Terhune published articles in several central California newspapers and magazines and successfully pitched numerous print, radio, and TV stories for clients. She completed internships with several corporate and nonprofit organizations, one of which turned into a public relations coordinator position with a nonprofit business incubator in Fresno, California. Terhune started her own public relations business at nineteen and maintained a varied client list, including high-end retail and Web 2.0 clients. In her last semester at Fresno State, she worked with three other students to launch and operate a completely student-operated public relations firm. Terhune served as the agency's first executive director, and under her leadership the firm grew to eighteen staff members and eight clients.

One of the few students to find a job in her desired industry prior to graduation, Terhune served as a guest lecturer to beginning public relations, public relations writing, and public relations entrepreneurship classes while still in school. Her expertise in the substance of this book was widely recognized on campus, and, as such, she was asked to share this knowledge with her peers.

Terhune is now the assistant marketing manager at Everloop, a social network built for kids under thirteen. Prior to Everloop, she was an account supervisor and social media specialist at 5 Rockets, Inc., a strategic Internet presence consultancy, where she created and managed social networks across multiple platforms.

Betsy A. Hays, APR, is a sought-after speaker, educator, and facilitator who specializes in communication and public relations topics, as well as the subject matter of this book. She is the lead public relations professor for the Department of Mass Communication and Journalism at California State University, Fresno, a post she has held since 1999. In addition to managing the public relations option, Professor Hays runs the internship and scholarship programs for the department. She is also the faculty advisor for the Public Relations Student Society of America, the Society for Latino Motivators, and the university's student-run PR firm.

Professor Hays earned her BA in journalism with an emphasis in public relations and her MA in mass communication from California State University, Fresno. Professor Hays is also an accredited public relations professional, having earned her APR designation from the Public Relations Society of America.

She has been involved in the public relations profession for more than twenty years, having worked full time in the field for eight years prior to beginning her university teaching career. During her early years of teaching, Professor Hays counseled some nonprofit clients on a pro bono basis, and in 2003 she opened her own consulting business. In addition, Professor Hays frequently conducts seminars and workshops to assist businesses and organizations in solid public relations practices, as well as media relations, presentation skills, social media strategies, and personal and professional branding.

Her research interests include public relations entrepreneurship, infusing entrepreneurship education into the collegiate public relations curriculum, and reverse mentoring in public relations. Her articles about these topics have been published in numerous academic journals.

She has served on the board of directors of the Central California Chapter of the Public Relations Society of America (PRSA) since 1998 and was its president in 1998 and 2010. Professor Hays is now in her third year on the board of directors for PRSA's North Pacific District. She was named PRSA's Public Relations Professional of the Year in 2000 and has also been honored with the prestigious Provost's Award for promising new tenure-track faculty at Fresno State. She created the nation's first-ever public relations entrepreneurship course in 2007 and is also the architect of fully integrating the pedagogy of service learning into the university's public relations program.

Prior to her service to Fresno State, Professor Hays worked for Deen & Black Public Relations (now Ogilvy Worldwide) and served as both media spokesperson and media trainer for clients throughout California and Arizona, mainly in the government sector. She has also coordinated a regional public education program with sixty-two cities in central California, helping cities spread the word about the importance of solid waste management. In addition, Professor Hays spent two years working in both internal and external public relations for Saint Agnes Medical Center in Fresno, California.

LIT
NCL

CPSIA information can be obtained at www.ICGtesting.com
Printed in the USA
BVOW03s2347090415

395529BV00001B/1/P

9 781442 219472